Y0-ADK-140

The *Pronunciation* of *Canadian French*

The *Pronunciation* of *Canadian French*

DOUGLAS C. WALKER

University of Ottawa Press
1984
Ministry of Education, Ontario
Information Centre, 13th Floor,
Mowat Block, Queen's Park,
Toronto, Ont.   M7A 1L2

CANADIAN CATALOGUING IN PUBLICATION DATA
Walker, Douglas C.
The Pronunciation of Canadian French

Bibliography: p.
ISBN 0-7766-4500-5

1. French language — Canada. 2. French language — Pronunciation. I. Title.

PC3615.W34 1984   448'.1   C84-090218-2

© University of Ottawa Press, Ottawa, Canada, 1984
ISBN 0-7766-4500-5
PRINTED AND BOUND IN CANADA

TABLE OF CONTENTS

Acknowledgements		xi
Notation and Abbreviations		xiii

Chapter 1 INTRODUCTION 3

Chapter 2 SURVEY OF STANDARD FRENCH PHONOLOGY 11

2.0	*Introduction*	11
2.1	*The vowel phonemes of SF*	13
2.1.1	*Schwa*	16
2.1.2	*Vowel Length*	19
2.1.3	*Constraints on the mid vowels*	22
2.1.4	*Nasalized vowels*	24
2.1.5	*Vowels and semi-vowels*	25
2.1.6	*Stress and syllabification*	27
2.2	*The consonant phonemes of SF*	31
2.2.1	*Consonant allophones*	32
2.2.2	*Varying realizations of /R/*	33
2.2.3	*Devoicing and voicing assimilation*	33
2.2.4	*Gaps in the consonant inventory*	36
2.2.5	*Modifications involving nasals*	37
2.2.6	*Aspirate*-h	38
2.2.7	*Final consonants*	40

Chapter 3 THE VOWEL SYSTEM OF CANADIAN FRENCH 45

3.0	*Introduction*	45
3.1	*Vowel length*	45
3.2	*Vowel laxing*	53
3.2.1	*Pretonic laxing*	57
3.2.2	*Laxing harmony*	61
3.3	*Diphthongization*	64
3.4	*Devoicing*	72
3.5	*Vowel deletion*	75

	3.6	*The low vowels /a/ and /ɑ/*	77
	3.7	*The lowering of /ɛ/*	84
	3.8	*The diphthong* oi	87
	3.9	*Nasalized vowels*	92
	3.10	*Schwa in CF*	94
	3.11	*Residual problems*	98
	3.12	*Summary and conclusions*	99
Chapter 4		THE CANADIAN FRENCH CONSONANT SYSTEM	105
	4.0	*Introduction*	105
	4.1	*Assibilation*	105
	4.2	*Final consonant deletion*	108
	4.3	*Final consonant retention or insertion*	111
	4.4	*Nasal assimilation*	113
	4.5	*Velarization of /ɲ/*	115
	4.6	*The phoneme /r/*	116
	4.7	*Residual or restricted phenomena*	116
	4.7.1	h	117
	4.7.2	*Mellowing*	117
	4.7.3	*Loss of /r/ and /l/*	118
	4.8	*Summary and conclusions*	119
Chapter 5		THE PROSODIC STRUCTURE OF CANADIAN FRENCH	123
	5.0	*Introduction*	123
	5.1	*Length*	123
	5.2	*Stress*	126
	5.3	*Tone*	128
	5.4	*Intonation*	130
Chapter 6		QUESTIONS OF CANADIAN FRENCH MORPHOPHONOLOGY	133
	6.0	*Introduction*	133
	6.1	*Simple pronoun subjects in CF*	135
	6.2	*Direct object pronouns*	138
	6.3	*Articles*	141
	6.4	*Complex cases: indirect objects, gemination, fusion, and other processes*	144

6.5	*Summary of rules*	149
6.6	*Remarks on CF morphology*	152
APPENDIX 1	*Phonological Features*	159
APPENDIX 2	*Glossary*	161
APPENDIX 3	*List of Rules*	169
BIBLIOGRAPHY		171

Acknowledgements

The description of Canadian French which follows is the product of a number of years of observation, sometimes systematic, often accidental, of a variety of French that presents an incredible richness of data relevant to the professional linguistic analyst and to the amateur alike. Virtually every aspect of discussion in current linguistic theory may be illustrated, debated and, frequently enough, contradicted on the basis of Canadian French material. Likewise, the language learner or the casual observer may be interested, challenged or frustrated in attempts to grapple with a form of the spoken language that has escaped systematic discussion in the technical or the non-technical literature. I hope that the information in the subsequent chapters will permit and encourage a closer contact with the sound system of Canada's official Romance language, as it is spoken and "lived", rather than as it reposes in normative textbooks. I must, consequently, acknowledge with thanks the assistance of students, colleagues and friends who have brought Canadian French alive for me, and who have contributed in large part to the improvement of the analysis and to its presentation in what follows. Three students, Dominique Bossé, France Martineau and Valérie Munn, commented on the manuscript in detail at various stages and gave me the benefit of their intuitions as native speakers. Janet Shorten of the University of Ottawa Press was most encouraging in the details of editorial "fine-tuning". Many colleagues, at one time or another, have discussed this material with me. I would like to thank specifically Pierre Calvé, André Lapierre, Shana Poplack and David Sankoff. I must also single out Noel Corbett who has influenced, in its form and its substance, every section of this book through his insightful comments and constructive disagreements. And finally, I would be remiss if I did not point out the stimulating and supportive environment of the Department of Linguistics at the University of Ottawa, a context that has done much to instruct me in the pleasures of work on Canadian French and on linguistics in general.

Notation and Abbreviations

Much of the material in this study is described using phonetic symbols and formal notational conventions. In order to facilitate the use of the book, this notation is presented here in some detail, with explanation and exemplification where necessary. Further information, including a list of the distinctive phonetic features and a glossary, is found in the Appendices.

(A) *Phonetic Notation*

1. Vowels

		front		central	back
high	tense	i	ü	ɨ	u
	lax	I	Ü		U
higher-mid		e	ø		o
				ə ʌ	
lower-mid		ɛ	œ		ɔ
low		æ		a	ɑ

Among the front vowels, the first member of each of the pairs i-ü, I-Ü, e-ø and ɛ-œ is unrounded, the second rounded.

Diacritic marks. The following symbols may be added to the representations of vowels to indicate additional properties (V = any vowel):

Ṽ	nasalized vowel
V̥	voiceless vowel
V:	long vowel
V́	primary stress
V̀	secondary stress

2. Semi-vowels (glides)

front unrounded	j
front rounded	ɥ
back rounded	w

3. Consonants

	bilabial	labio-dental	inter-dental	apical	palatal	velar	uvular	glottal
stop	p b			t d	c ɟ	k g		ʔ
fricative	φ β	f v	θ ð	s z	ʃ ʒ	x γ		h
affricate		pf		tˢdᶻ	č ǰ	kˣ		
flaps/trills				ř r̃			R	
nasals	m			n	ɲ	ŋ		
laterals				l	ʎ	ɫ		

Among the pairs of stops, fricatives and affricates, the first member is voiceless, the second voiced.

Diacritic marks. The following symbols may be added to the representations of consonants to indicate additional properties (C = any consonant):

    C̥   voiceless consonant (when C is normally voiced)
    C̦   voiced consonant (when C is normally voiceless)
    C: long or geminate consonant
    C̩   syllabic consonant
    C̃   fronted consonant
    Cʰ   aspirated consonant
    Cʲ   palatalized consonant

(B) *The phonemic system of General Canadian English*

1. VOWELS, SEMI-VOWELS AND DIPHTHONGS

i		u	j	w	aj	aw
I		U				ɔj
e	əʌ	o				
ɛ		ɔ				
æ	a					

Examples:
i   b*ea*t
I   b*i*t
e   b*ai*t
ɛ   b*e*t
æ   b*a*t
u   b*oo*t
U   b*oo*k
o   b*oa*t
ɔ   b*ou*ght
a   b*a*r, b*a*lance
ə   *a*bove, sof*a*
ʌ   ab*o*ve, c*u*t
j   *y*et
w   *w*et
aj   b*uy*
aw   b*ough*
ɔj   b*oy*

2. Consonants

	p		t	č	k	
	b		d	ǰ	g	
		f θ	s	ʃ		h
		v ð	z	ʒ		
m			n		ŋ	
			l	r		

Examples:

p	*p*in
b	*b*in
t	*t*in
d	*d*in
č	*ch*in
ǰ	*g*in
k	*k*in
g	*g*un
f	*f*un
v	*v*an
θ	*th*in
ð	*th*en
s	*s*in
z	*z*oo
ʃ	*sh*in
ʒ	mea*s*ure
m	*m*oon
n	*n*oon
ŋ	ru*ng*
l	*l*ung
r	*r*ung

(C) *The phonemic system of Standard French*

1. VOWELS AND SEMI-VOWELS

i	ü		u				j ɥ w
e	ø		o				
ɛ	œ	ə	ɔ				
				ɛ̃	œ̃		ɔ̃
		a	ɑ			ɑ̃	

Examples:
i	v*i*e
ü	v*u*e
u	v*ou*s
e	n*é*
ø	cr*eu*x
o	h*au*t
ɛ	s*e*lle
œ	s*eu*l
ɔ	s*o*tte
ə	pr*e*mier
a	p*a*tte
ɑ	p*â*te
ɛ̃	v*in*
œ̃	br*un*
ɔ̃	b*on*
ɑ̃	b*an*c
j	pa*ill*e
ɥ	h*u*it
w	*ou*ate

2. Consonants

	p		t		k	
	b		d		g	
		f	s	ʃ		
		v	z	ʒ		
	m		n	ɲ	ŋ	
			l			R

Examples:
p	*p*ont
b	*b*on
t	*t*on
d	*d*ont
k	*c*amp
g	*g*ant
f	*f*ont
v	*v*ont
s	*s*ont
z	*z*one
ʃ	*ch*ou
ʒ	*j*our
m	*m*on
n	*n*ous
ɲ	beig*n*e
ŋ	parki*ng*
l	*l*oup
R	*r*oue

Additional features of Canadian French (not necessarily phonemic):

I	f*i*ls
Ü	j*u*pe
U	c*ou*pe
ɛː	gu*ê*pe
tˢ	*t*u
dᶻ	*d*ire
č	*ch*um
ǰ	*j*ob
ř/r̃	*r*ond

For the complete set of phonological features used to describe and to classify these and other sounds, see Appendix 1.

(D) *Formal notational devices*

[ ]	square brackets enclose a phonetic transcription or (sets of) phonological features
/ /	slant lines enclose phonemic transcriptions
→	the arrow indicates "becomes, is rewritten as, is realized as". Thus, A → B is an abbreviation for "A is realized as B".
/ _	used to indicate the environment where changes occur. Thus, A → B/C _ D abbreviates "A is realized as B when preceded by C and followed by D". Either C or D may be absent. For example, V → Ṽ/ _ N is read as "vowels become nasalized when followed by nasal consonants".
C	any consonant; segments which are [–syllabic]
V	any vowel; segments which are [+ syllabic]

L   any liquid, i.e. "l" or "r" type sounds, as in *l*ip or *r*ip.

G   any glide or semi-vowel; j ɥ w; segments which are $\begin{bmatrix} -\text{syllabic} \\ -\text{consonantal} \end{bmatrix}$

N   any nasal consonant

X   a variable standing for any arbitrary sequence of phonological material. Thus, a formula V → V: / _ NX is read as "vowels become long before nasal consonants no matter what follows the nasal consonant".

*   indicates an impossible, non-occurring or ungrammatical form. Thus, *Ṽ V means the sequence of a nasal vowel preceding a vowel may not occur.

∅   the null element (not to be confused with ø, a higher-mid front rounded vowel) indicates that material is inserted or deleted. Thus, N → ∅/Ṽ _ # means that nasal consonants are deleted following nasalized vowels, while ∅ → G/V _ # means that glides are inserted following vowels.

$ syllable boundary. Thus, _ C$ means "before a consonant which precedes a syllable boundary".

\#   word boundary. ∅ → e / # _ C means "insert *e* at the beginning of words in front of a word-initial consonant".

X_0^1 subscript numerals indicate the minimum number of segments of type X necessary for a process to take place; superscripts indicate the maximum permissible. Thus, V → ∅ / _ C_1^2 indicates that a vowel is deleted when followed by at least one and at most two consonants.

( ) parentheses enclose optional material. Thus, A(B)C abbreviates the two sequences ABC and AC. In the formula V → Ṽ / _ (#)N, a vowel may be nasalized before a following nasal consonant in either the presence or the absence of an intervening word boundary.

{ } curly brackets enclose optional choices in the same position. Thus, V → Ø / _ $\begin{Bmatrix} C_2 \\ \# \end{Bmatrix}$ means that vowels are deleted either before two consonants or before a word boundary.

α, β alpha variables are variables ranging over the feature values + and −, and are used to indicate agreement in distinctive features. Thus, Ø → $\begin{bmatrix} G \\ \alpha\text{ round} \end{bmatrix}$ / _ $\begin{bmatrix} V \\ \alpha\text{ round} \end{bmatrix}$ means "insert a glide agreeing in rounding with the following vowel". (Vowel and glide must both be either [+round] or [−round]: /ji/ and /wu/ are acceptable, but /ju/ is not.)

/ a line through a letter indicates that the letter is not pronounced: *petit/*, *capabl/*.

These notational devices may be combined to indicate relatively complex processes. Consider the following, based on actual rules taken from the literature:

(a)   V → [+stress] / _ $C_0 \begin{bmatrix} V \\ -\text{tense} \end{bmatrix} C_0^1 \, V \, C_0 \#$

The third vowel from the end of the word is stressed, provided that the second vowel from the end of the word is lax ([−tense]) and is followed by no more than one consonant. (The two symbols "C_0" mean that any number of consonants may occur in those positions.)

(b)   V → [−syllabic] / # _ $\begin{bmatrix} +\text{syllabic} \\ +\text{high} \end{bmatrix}$

Vowels become glides when they occur preceding high vowels at the beginning of words.

Each of these notational devices will be illustrated in the CF material to follow.

The *Pronunciation* of *Canadian French*

CHAPTER 1

Introduction

All languages vary along geographic, social or temporal dimensions. While there may exist varying degrees of resistance to change (Icelandic comes immediately to mind as a typically conservative example), and varying reactions to regional and social variation, it is clear that "French" is entirely typical as regards the heterogeneity which the term denotes. Regional and social dialects are manifest both within continental France and in a broader international setting. This variation exists even within the limits of what has become known as "standard" or "international" or "general" French, as much recent work (Martinet and Walter 1973, for example) makes clear. In this context, the French spoken in Canada is simply another regional variety of an international language—a variety that must confront the typical political, economic and social pressures that regional and minority languages face, and that are more than evident in contemporary Quebec. The chapters that follow will present a general survey of the phonological and morphophonological properties of Canadian French.

But Canadian French is no less immune to the diversification that touches every speech community. Even leaving aside the speech of Western Canada or of the Maritimes, it is evident that the French of Quebec is highly diversified. (Dulong and Bergeron 1980 indicate this in geographical terms, while much of the work dealing with the Sankoff-Cedergren corpus demonstrates the social stratification of Quebec French.) It is not misleading, however, to say (as does Brent 1970:117) that the major linguistic variation within Quebec is along social rather than geographic lines. In social terms, one may recognize a gamut of styles in Canadian French that range between speech virtually indistinguishable from the Parisian norm to that clearly unmonitored and colloquial variant that has been both stigmatized and hailed—*le joual*. And even in the latter case, there is no unanimity of opinion as to what the term represents. In any event, any work purporting to describe Canadian French must be more precise in defining the object of its attention.

Clearly, we can eliminate from the outset a too formal style—a style that rapidly approximates Standard French and is more than adequately described in numerous manuals (such as Fouché 1959, Martinet 1945 or Walter 1976). We will concentrate instead on an informal or colloquial style of Canadian French: the popular speech of Montreal, which is amply documented in a wide variety of reports, many of which are based on the fundamentally important corpus established by Sankoff and Cedergren, and which is broadly representative of the style in question. We will also include, in passing, remarks on characteristics of the French spoken in Quebec that are not restricted to Montreal, nor even particularly frequent in that city, but which are widely known and which form part of the general "linguistic folklore" of Quebec. Nevertheless, the primary focal point of the description to follow will be the popular speech of Montreal, corresponding to the general popular French that is described by Bauche 1920, Frei 1929 and, more recently, Morin 1979. The parallel between popular Canadian French and popular Parisian French is deliberate, in that it illustrates both the level of language to be described and the obvious similarities to be found in the two dialects.

The descriptive material which follows is organized into five parts. Chapter 2 presents a brief survey of the phonology of Standard French. The inclusion of this material is a reflection of practical and of comparative goals, and should not be seen as reflecting judgements of priority or of relative value. The fact remains, however, that many individuals have at least a passive knowledge of the phonology of Standard French which it will be useful to review before addressing the Canadian French material. It is also useful to recall that even Standard French includes considerable variation, and that a monolithic, homogeneous, invariant notion "French" corresponds to no linguistic reality. Finally, it will also be evident that many of the innovations in Canadian French represent extensions of phenomena that are already present in the "reference point" (i.e. Standard French) and that a knowledge of the standard dialect will help clarify many of the phonological properties of the Canadian variety.

Following the overview of Standard French, subsequent chapters treat the Canadian French vowel system, consonant system, prosody, and certain aspects of the link between phonology and morphology. Of these four, the first and the last are by far the longest, reflecting both the degree of difference between the two dialects and the dimensions of the scholarly literature which deals with the phenomena in question. In particular, the vowel system presents significant differences from continental French, both in the structure of the system itself and in the phonetic realizations of the various elements. The contrast between strengthened (lengthened, diphthongized) allophones and weakened variants (laxed, devoiced, deleted) is particularly noticeable. In the consonant domain, there are far fewer differences of paradigmatic structure, whereas the allophonic variation and the insertion or deletion of consonants in specific lexical items is of greater importance. The little firm knowledge available concerning the prosodic system links Canadian French fairly directly to the standard, while the morphophonemic evidence shows both similarity to aspects of popular French and a significant set of Canadian innovations.

Such innovations are not the only interesting property manifested by Canadian French. It is, of course, always relevant to explore the structure of a particular dialect, and to add to our knowledge of French dialectology in general, a vast domain that has so heavily influenced, since Gillieron, the way in which we conceive of language and of linguistic change. But in addition to its intrinsic interest, study of Canadian French has certain practical benefits for the teaching of the language. Many current approaches to language teaching concentrate on oral comprehension and production. Whether or not specifically Canadian characteristics are to form part of a person's active, productive competence (and this will no doubt remain controversial, given that Canadian traits are found most heavily in popular or colloquial speech), it is clear that in the Canadian, and even international, context, learners will be constantly exposed to popular and to Canadian accents. It can only be a service to language learners to increase their flexibility by permitting them familiarity, at least passively, with spoken Canadian French. The systematic overview of the phonology of that dialect presented in what follows should contribute to the material available for teaching French in the Canadian context.

Finally, we may note that the diverse properties of Canadian French are of considerable theoretical relevance. Many of its phonetic attributes are of striking interest on typological grounds: nasalized vowels, voiceless vowels, the interplay between laxing and diphthongization all provide fascinating data. In more abstract terms, questions of vowel harmony, the role of word boundaries, types of morphophonemic innovation, and the interaction between various types of rules furnish material for current theoretical debates. Nor should it be necessary to emphasize the contribution that Canadian French studies have made and can continue to make to sociolinguistics. Virtually every question of sociolinguistic theory can be illustrated with Canadian data; in what follows we will have ample opportunity to discuss and illustrate variable rules, and the factors that influence the implementation of phonological and morphophonemic rules.

Such questions have preoccupied many investigators of Canadian French in the past decade. It was not always the case, however, and observers have more than once been moved to comment on a certain parochialism in Canadian French linguistics. Corbett 1975: 380 noted in this respect that "c'est aussi pourquoi cette linguistique, à intérêt surtout local, tend d'un côté à mettre au premier plan les données concrètes et les problèmes pratiques, de l'autre, à rejeter à l'arrière plan la théorie." For a variety of reasons, the "données concrètes" of earlier studies were largely limited to the phonetic and lexicographical domains. Nor was it the case that general or theoretically oriented surveys formed part of the first rank of studies. (Vinay 1973 and Walker 1979 offer certain comments on this situation.) Again, it is to be hoped that the present work will contribute to a growing body of work that seeks to insert Canadian French studies into a broader context, to the mutual benefit of both descriptive work and the domain of phonological theory.

Contemporary linguistics is resolutely descriptive in its outlook, and the work to follow will share that point of view. Of course one can, and must, on occasion, make value judgements about language and its use. But such judgements are made on the basis of non-linguistic factors, factors which are inserted into a complex and highly structured social-psychological network. These judgements, moreover, are often more symptomatic of the attitudes of the evaluator than of any inherent property of the language in question. In other contexts, however, certain pronouncements about the nature of Canadian French demonstrate a profound ignorance of the inherent properties of language. Such is the case with claims that "Le soi-disant québécois est un langage sans vocabulaire arrêté, sans règles grammaticales, sans syntaxe, sans exigences d'aucune sorte" ("Manifeste contre le joual," *La Presse*, Feb. 9, 1973) or "Parler joual c'est parler franglais, c'est parler un français qui ne se tient pas, qui est sans syntaxe, sans phonétique, sans grammaire, sans règles" (Television broadcast "La langue au Québec"). Such statements mistake differences in rules for absence of rules, and ignore the incredibly rich structures, processes and relations that are part and parcel of Quebec French, as they are of any language. In fact, the spontaneous, unmonitored level of speech may be *more* regular than formal styles, as Labov et al. 1972 note in their major study of sound change in progess: "this vernacular [the linguistic style or register in which the minimum degree of attention is paid to speech] is the most systematic form of language, and... more formal styles produce in most speakers irregular and unpredictable distributions..." (1972:3). To an exemplification and a discussion of such regularities in Quebec French phonology, we now cast our attention, following a brief survey of the standard French background.

FURTHER READING—INTRODUCTION

Following each chapter, we will indicate a limited number of works, organized thematically, which may be used as an introduction to further study of the material in question. As far as the introductory chapter is concerned, the following general manuals, chosen from a multitude of possibilities, present a survey of the fundamental principles of descriptive linguistics:
>Bloomfield (1933)
>Fromkin and Rodman (1983)
>Hockett (1965)
>Lyons (1968)
>Martinet (1964)

Historical linguistics, dialectology and sociolinguistics may be approached via:
>Bynon (1977)
>Chambers and Trudgill (1980)
>Labov (1972)

(Anttila 1972, while more technical, is an excellent survey of historical and comparative linguistics).

General introductions to current phonological theory include:
>Chomsky and Halle (1968)
>Dell (1980)
>Fischer-Jørgensen (1975)
>Hooper (1976)
>Hyman (1975)
>Schane (1973)
>Sommerstein (1977)

(Of these, Schane is the most elementary; Chomsky and Halle, and Hooper, are the most technical.)

General syntheses of Canadian French are rare. The following present important information, often restricted to specific areas, but useful for an understanding of the broader setting of CF studies.

>Bouthillier and Meynard (1972)—social and historical commentary
>Brent (1970)
>Charbonneau (1955)
>Gendron (1966a)—standard reference for general phonological survey of CF
>Juneau (1972)—historical phonology
>Léon (1968)
>Orkin (1967)—a non-technical, popularizing survey
>Santerre (1976a)

CHAPTER 2

Survey of Standard French Phonology

2.0 *Introduction*

Before discussing those phonological properties most characteristic of Canadian French (CF), it is necessary to set the background by considering briefly the phonological system of Standard French (SF). There are several reasons for this. First, SF is of course one of the variants of the French language spoken in Canada, though not the one that is the focus of this book. As one normative variant, it has gained a broad exposure, given its role in the school system, in the mass media and so on. It is also highly likely that among second language learners, the normative approach to language teaching has had the standard language as its target.

For our purposes, however, there is a better reason for a survey of SF. Accepting the great degree of familiarity with SF among both French and English speakers (the overwhelming majority of *Québecois* are at least passively in contact with SF as realized in the media, for example), it provides an excellent point of reference from which to appreciate the innovations that have taken place in the North American context. Many CF modifications, in other words, take on a particularly interesting structure and theoretical import when viewed through an SF prism.

It will on occasion be necessary to introduce a certain amount of technical information into what follows. In particular, many notions of current phonological theory are relevant to a discussion of any phonological system. Each time more technical information is necessary, it will be discussed and exemplified in the text. (No detailed discussion of phonology can be given here, in a discussion that is oriented toward a description of CF, not toward phonological theory. Further information is contained in the suggested readings.) But underlying the whole presentation is the fundamental distinction between phonetic versus phonological representation, the former enclosed in square backets, [ ]; the latter in slant lines, / /.

Phonetic representations are detailed technical descriptions intended to represent all possible characteristics of sound difference, including detail that is never relevant (distinctive) in the language in question. Phonological representations, on the other hand, retain only distinctive information—that on which the message may depend. The difference between phonetic (allophonic) detail and distinctive (phonological) information may be seen in the following example from English. In English, the letter *l* may represent at least two radically different types of sounds, a so-called "clear l" in syllable-initial position (at the beginning of words and in front of vowels), contrasted with a "dark l" in syllable-final position (at the end of words and in front of consonants). Consider the English words in (1):

(1)   (a) "clear l"   (b) "dark l"

*l*ift	[lIft]	—	pi*ll*	[pɨł]
*l*eap	[lIjp]	—	mi*l*e	[majł]
a*l*one	[əlówn]	—	mi*l*k	[mɨłk]
re*l*y	[rəláj]	—	fi*l*ter	[fɨłtər]

Phonetically speaking, it is necessary to recognize the difference between [l] and [ł]. But this difference is never distinctive in English; one can always predict on the basis of context whether one is to have [l] (syllable-initially) or [ł] (syllable-finally and preceding consonants). A phonological description, therefore, would ignore this irrelevant detail, and would represent both types of sound with the same symbol in a phonological representation: /lIft/ and /pIl/, /rəlaj/ and /fIltər/ etc.

In technical terms, [l] and [ł] constitute two *allophones* of a single /l/ *phoneme*, and it is among the tasks of phonology to specify all the allophones or possible realizations of the set of phonemes of a language. This is usually done in terms of allophonic rules, illustrated in the present case by the formula in (2):

SURVEY OF STANDARD FRENCH PHONOLOGY

(2) /l/ → $\begin{cases} [ɫ] \,/\, \_\,\$, C \\ [l] \text{ elsewhere} \end{cases}$

The formula (2) is to be interpreted as saying that the phoneme /l/ in English has two allophones, [ɫ] occurring in syllable-final or preconsonantal position and [l] everywhere else. In our comparison of SF and CF phonology, we will be constantly concerned with a discussion of the phonemic inventories of the two dialects, and of the allophonic realizations of the phonemes. We will at the same time be concerned with the way that phonemes may be combined in the formation of words.[1]

2.1   The vowel phonemes of SF

Compared with many languages, SF contains a very rich vocalic inventory. The vowel system is diagrammed in (3).

(3)   SF VOWELS

high	i	ü		u
higher-mid	e	ø	ə	o
lower-mid	ɛ	œ		ɔ
low			a	ɑ
	front		back	

In addition, we must consider three semi-vowels corresponding to the high vowels, and four nasalized vowels:

(4)   Semi vowels: j   ɥ   w

   Nasalized vowels: ɛ̃   œ̃   ɑ̃   ɔ̃

These segments are given more detailed specifications in terms of distinctive features in (5) below:

---

1. For further discussion of the phonemic-allophonic distinction, and of phonology in general, see Fischer-Jørgensen 1975 and the references of Appendix I.

(5) DISTINCTIVE FEATURE COMPOSITION OF SF VOWELS AND SEMI-VOWELS

	i	ü	u	e	ø	o	ɛ	œ	ə	ɔ	a	ɑ	ɛ̃	œ̃	ɑ̃	ɔ̃	j	ɥ	w
syllabic	+	+	+	+	+	+	+	+	+	+	+	+	+	+	+	+	−	−	−
high	+	+	+	+	+	+	−	−	−	−	−	−	−	−	−	−	+	+	+
mid	−	−	−	+	+	+	+	+	+	+	−	−	+	+	−	+	−	−	−
back	−	−	+	−	−	+	−	−	−	+	−	+	−	−	+	+	−	−	+
round	−	+	+	−	+	+	−	+	−	+	−	−	−	+	−	+	−	+	+
tense	+	+	+	+	+	+	+	+	−	+	+	+	+	+	+	+	+	+	+
nasal	−	−	−	−	−	−	−	−	−	−	−	−	+	+	+	+	−	−	−

Before any further discussion, let us exemplify each vowel in various contexts, including stressed and unstressed position and open and closed syllables (open syllables end in a vowel, closed syllables in a consonant). It is a strong tendency of SF to maintain open syllabification. One immediate consequence of this is that VCV sequences are syllabified V$CV, where "$" represents the syllable boundary. In (6a), as a consequence, the vowels of the first syllable are in open position. In addition, note that stress in SF falls on the last syllable of the word, unless that vowel is schwa ('mute e'), in which case the preceding syllable is stressed. Consequently, the italicized vowels of (6a) and (6c) are stressed.

In addition to the relatively large number of vowels in this system (compared to many other languages—Spanish, for instance, which has only /i e a o u/), we may note the presence of two typologically rare groups: front rounded and nasalized vowels. What, then, are the general properties of the SF system? We will study those that are most important for an understanding of the CF developments.

We should note first that all SF vowels, with the exception of schwa (mute-e) are considered to be tense; that is, produced with heightened muscular tension, a considerable degree of displacement toward the periphery of the oral cavity, and a greater duration than their lax partners. Unlike their English counterparts, the SF vowels are not diphthongized.

(6) EXAMPLES OF SF VOWELS IN VARIOUS CONTEXTS

	(a) *stressed open*	(b) *unstressed open*	(c) *stressed closed*	(d) *unstressed closed*
i	pol*i*	f*i*nesse	v*i*te	f*i*ltrage
e	f*ée*	pr*é*dire	—	—
ɛ	m*ais*	m*aî*tresse	f*ê*te	f*e*stival
ü	cr*u*	br*u*tal	fl*û*te	p*u*rger
ø	f*eu*	j*eu*di	j*eû*ne*	h*eu*r*eu*sement
œ	—	j*eu*nesse	p*eu*r	h*eu*rter
u	cl*ou*	cl*ou*ter	v*oû*te	f*ou*rmi
o	b*eau*	b*eau*té	s*au*te	h*au*tement
ɔ	—	b*o*tté*	s*o*tte	p*o*rtage
a	m*a*	*a*ssumer	pl*a*te	*a*lpin
ɑ	m*ât*	b*â*ton	p*â*te	b*a*ssement
ə	—*	cr*e*ver	—	—
ɛ̃	f*ein*t	p*ein*ture	cr*ain*te	p*in*cement
œ̃	br*un*	empr*un*ter	déf*un*te	*un* de ces...*
ɔ̃	bl*on*d	b*on*dir	r*on*de	l*on*guement
ɑ̃	bl*an*c	bl*an*chir	pl*an*te	ch*an*gement

(e) semi-vowels *

		#__	C__	V__
j		*y*oga	p*i*ed	pa*ill*e
ɥ		h*u*it	p*u*is	—
w		*ou*i	p*oi*ds	—

---

* Items marked with an asterisk are discussed in the text below. This table takes into account the dropping of "mute *e*" in creating certain contexts. In addition, the notation "#" stands for word boundary, and "C", "V" for any consonant or vowel respectively.

2.1.1 *Schwa*

The only lax vowel, schwa, has long been considered a problem, both because its phonetic properties are not well understood and because of the particularly complicated set of conditions determining its deletion. To begin with, schwa in standard dialects is now often merged phonetically with one of the two front rounded vowels [ø] or [œ]. When stressed, in particular, it is often [ø]: *sur ce* [sürsǿ]; *prenez-le* [prœnelǿ]. When unstressed, schwa varies according to as yet little understood factors. For Dell 1980, for example, *prenait* is pronounced [prœnɛ], not [prənɛ]. Given this merger, the only way of distinguishing mute-*e* is now through its phonological behaviour; some instances of [œ] will act as mute-*e*, and will delete; others will remain stable. Consider the difference between (7a) and (7b), which illustrate the difference between two types of [œ].

(7)   (a)   *vous secouez*   *elle secouait*
               /vuskue/   /ɛlsœkwɛ/

               vous remuez   *Jacques remuait*
               /vurmüe/   /ʒakrœmɥɛ/

      (b)   *vous rajeunissez*   *elle rajeunissait*
               /vuraʒœnise/   /ɛlraʒœnise/
               */raʒnise/

               il m'écoeurait   *elle m'écoeurait*
               /imekœrɛ/   /ɛlmekœrɛ/
               */mekrɛ/

In the (a) forms, we see examples of [œ] which may be deleted in certain contexts; in (b), the phonetically identical segment may never drop. The precise means of distinguishing between "unstable [œ]" and "stable [œ]" go beyond the bounds of this work (see, in particular, the excellent discussion in Dell 1980, Part II). We will simply note this problem as a further difficulty associated with mute-*e* in SF and will continue to represent it as /ə/. We should, in addition, note that schwa is subject to a number of conditions in modern French. It may not occur in word-initial position, nor adjacent to a vowel within words, nor in closed syllables, nor under stress. Thus, /pəti/ 'petit', /kao/ 'chaos' and so on are possible SF words, but */əti/, */kəo/, */mətla/, */lə́/ are not.[2] Finally, note that in informal speech, there is a strong tendency to delete as many mute-*e* as possible (subject to various constraints), in contradistinction to more formal styles. Compare the realizations in (8).

(8) *Il venait de m'en donner quatre.*
 (a) /ivnɛdmɑ̃dɔnekat/
 (b) /ilvənɛdəmɑ̃dɔnekatrə/

While both pronunciations are theoretically possible, the second is much more formal, and would never occur in colloquial, informal conversation. It is not possible to cover here the incredibly complex situation regarding the deletion of schwa in SF. We will merely sketch the major areas of concern. To begin with, we will identify three major positions: phrase-final, phrase-initial and medial syllables. The very rough generalizations we can make are illustrated in (9).

(9) (a) Phrase-final (pre-pausal) schwas delete:

   j'en ai quatre
   ferme la porte
   au centre ville
   c'est mon père

---

2. The asterisk in this context indicates an impossible or non-occurring form. We omit, in this discussion, certain exceptional forms involving the "h-aspiré": *le héros* /ləero/, *rehausser* /rəose/, as well as the consequences of stressing *le* in certain limited morphological constructions (*dites-le*). Certain differences in CF are taken up in the next chapter.

(b) Schwas in initial syllables are often retained, especially following stop consonants:

> que faites vous
> revenez nous voir
> te fais pas de bile
> levez-vous

Schwas may be dropped, however, in certain expressions, particularly involving *je* or other highly recurrent and familiar words. The behaviour here is particularly variable and heterogeneous:

> j∅ viens d'arriver
> j∅ sais ce que tu veux
> j∅ pars demain
> c∅ que...
> c∅ qui...
> c∅pendant

(Note, however, the retention of schwa in c*e*lui, and in c*e*ci at the beginning of phrases.)

(c) Schwas in medial syllables delete if no more than one consonant precedes:

> méd∅cin   vs orphelin
> sam∅di   vs parvenir
> le r∅tour   vs chaque retour
> la s∅maine   vs cette semaine
> nous r∅gagnons vs Jacques regagnait

When consecutive syllables contain schwa, at most every alternate schwa can be deleted:

> vous r∅venez or vous rev∅nez
> but not : *vous r∅v∅nez
> il voulait me∅ le d∅mander or
> il voulait me l∅ demander
> but not : *il voulait m∅ l∅ demander or
> il voulait me l∅ d∅mander etc.

SURVEY OF STANDARD FRENCH PHONOLOGY

(Deletion in adjacent syllables in such cases would produce impermissible consonant sequences: */rvn/, */mld/ and so on.)

Next, we should note an interesting rhythmic constraint in compound words. When the second member of the compound is monosyllabic, the schwa is retained; if the second item is bi- or polysyllabic, the schwa is deleted. In this way, a tri-syllabic word with a strong-weak-strong accentual pattern is produced, as in (10).

(10) porte-feuille   — port∅-monnaie
      garde-robe   — gard∅-malade
      porte-plume   — port∅-crayon
      garde-port   — gard∅-rivière
      porte-voix   — port∅-parole

Finally, there exists a tendency in informal speech to insert (or retain) a schwa at the end of words terminating in two consonants when the following item begins with a consonant:

(11) *ours blanc*   — /ursəblɑ̃/   "*ourse blanc*"
      arc boutant   — /arkəbutɑ̃/   "*arque boutant*"
      film polonais — /filməpɔlonɛ/ "*filme polonais*"
      T-shirt jaune — /tiʃœrtəʒon/ "*T-shirte jaune*"

Here, as elsewhere in the discussion of schwa, we should remember the considerable variability of phonological behaviour, the role of stylistic, frequency, phonotactic and even individual factors in determining the heterogeneous structure of this particularly complex process.

2.1.2 *Vowel length*

Let us now turn to a process of lengthening which produces two allophones for each SF vowel (except /ə/): a long and a short. Basically, there are two major causes of lengthening in SF. Certain vowels, called inherently long, are always long in closed syllables. Other vowels may be long if the syllable in which they occur is closed by a so-called "consonne allongeante." The inherently long vowels are /ø o ɑ/ and the nasal vowels. Whenever they occur in closed, stressed (final) syllabes, they will be longer than the same vowel in open syllables. Consider the vowels in (12):

(12) INHERENTLY LONG VOWELS [3]

	_C$			_$	
ø	jeûne	[ʒø:n]	jeu	[ʒø]
o	saute	[so:t]	sot	[so]
o	hausse	[o:s]	haut	[o]
ɑ	pâte	[pɑ:t]	pas	[pɑ]
ɑ	mâle	[mɑ:l]	mât	[mɑ]
ɛ̃	sainte	[sɛ̃:t]	saint	[sɛ̃]
ɛ̃	crainte	[krɛ̃:t]	craint	[krɛ̃]
œ̃	emprunte	[ãprœ̃:t]	emprunt	[ãprœ̃]
œ̃	défunte	[defœ̃:t]	défunt	[defœ̃]
ɔ̃	honte	[ɔ̃:t]	bon	[bɔ̃]
ɔ̃	compte	[kɔ̃:t]	don	[dɔ̃]
ã	vente	[vã:t]	vent	[vã]
ã	plante	[plã:t]	plan	[plã]

The second type of long vowel is found in (stressed, final) syllables which are closed by one of the "consonnes allongeantes": /v z ʒ r/ or the sequence /vr/. Consider the forms in (13), where [+length] indicates the presence of one of the lengthening consonants /v z ʒ r/ following the vowel.

---

3. In what follows, "$" represents a syllable boundary. In the configuration _C$, therefore, the vowel will be followed by a consonant in the same syllable, and that syllable will be closed. "_$", on the other hand, represents open syllables. For reasons which will become clear below, there are exceedingly few examples of /ø/ in closed syllables.

(13) LONG VOWELS BEFORE LENGTHENING CONSONANTS, SHORT VOWELS BEFORE NON-LENGTHENING CONSONANTS OR IN FINAL POSITION

		$\_\begin{bmatrix} C \\ +\text{length} \end{bmatrix}$		$\_\begin{bmatrix} C \\ -\text{length} \end{bmatrix}$		$\_\$$
i	*vivre*	[vi:vr]	*ville*	[vil]	*vie*	[vi]
i	*vise*	[vi:z]	*vice*	[vis]	*rit*	[ri]
ɛ	*paire*	[pɛ:r]	*peine*	[pɛn]	*mais*	[mɛ]
ɛ	*rêve*	[rɛ:v]	*veste*	[vɛst]	*fait*	[fɛ]
a	*rage*	[ra:ʒ]	*nappe*	[nap]	*chat*	[ʃa]
a	*cave*	[ka:v]	*chasse*	[ʃas]	*ta*	[ta]
u	*rouge*	[ru:ʒ]	*rousse*	[rus]	*vous*	[vu]
u	*pour*	[pu:r]	*poule*	[pul]	*poux*	[pu]
ɔ	*port*	[pɔ:r]	*sotte*	[sɔt]	—	
ɔ	*dort*	[dɔ:r]	*molle*	[mɔl]	—	
ü	*juge*	[ʒü:ʒ]	*cruche*	[krüʃ]	*cru*	[krü]
ü	*excuse*	[ɛkskü:z]	*jupe*	[ʒüp]	*jus*	[ʒü]
œ	*oeuvre*	[œ:vr]	*guele*	[gœl]	—	
œ	*fleuve*	[flœ:v]	*tilleul*	[tijœl]	—	

Needless to say, the inherently long vowels of (12) will also be long in any syllable closed by a lengthening consonant, as in *rose* [ro:z], *heureuse* [œrø:z], *change* [ʃɑ̃:ʒ], *croire* [krwɑ:r] and so on.

As a final detail in the discussion of vowel length in SF, we must mention a peripheral case where, in certain styles or with certain speakers, there remains a phonemic difference between long and short ɛ – /ɛ/ versus /ɛ:/.[4] This opposition may occur in a few pairs of words, such as those in (14), although not all speakers differentiate these forms consistently, and the difference is not marked in standard normative dictionaires (i.e. Warnant 1968).

---

4. As we will see in Chapter 3, section 3.1, the difference between [a] and [ɑ] / [ɑ:] is basically one of quality, not length, as can be demonstrated in final position where both vowels become short: *patte*, *pâte*, *le pas*, *ne... pas*: [pat – pɑ:t – ləpɑ – nəpɑ].

(14)   PHONEMIC DIFFERENCE BETWEEN /ɛ/ AND /ɛ:/ IN SF

/ɛ/	/ɛ:/
bette	bête
mettre	maître
faites	fête
lettre	l'être

2.1.3   Constraints on the mid vowels

There are several constraints in SF governing the contexts in which the pairs of vowels /e-ɛ/, /ø-œ/, /o-ɔ/ may occur. Such constraints are responsible for certains gaps in the sets of examples in (5) and (13) above. We will not discuss these constraints in great detail, but will sketch their general nature. The conditions on the vowel pairs crucially involve the notion of syllable structure, and reflect a tendency (sometimes called the "loi de position") for the vowels /e ø o/ to occur in open syllables, while /ɛ œ ɔ/ are found in closed syllables. This tendency is best illustrated in unstressed (i.e. non-final) syllables, where we find examples such as those in (15).

(15)   (a) *Unstressed open syllables*   (b) *Unstressed closed syllables*

	e	bêtise	ɛ	festival
	e	séchoir	ɛ	médecin
	ø	peuplier	œ	pleurnicher
	ø	pleuvoir	œ	flirter
	o	frôler	ɔ	costal
	o	beauté	ɔ	porter

Furthermore, this tendency is strongest in the closed syllables; in open position, for a variety of reasons,[5] it is possible to find both

---

5. These reasons include morphological relatedness—/fɛte/ *fêter* because of *fête*, /fɛt/, /bɔte/ *botté* because of /bɔt/ *botte* and so on, as well as the effects of vowel harmony—/depeʃe-depeʃe/ *dépêcher*, /sede-sedɛ/ *céder-cédait*, etc.

higher-mid and lower-mid vowels, as the more formal realizations /fɛte/ *fêter*, /brɔde/ *broder* attest. It is, in fact, easy to find /ɔ/ in pretonic open syllables; what we do not find is a distinctive difference between /ɔ/ and /o/, /ɛ/ and /e/ in this position, where the difference between the higher-mid and lower-mid vowels is said to be neutralized. (We must exclude such rare cases as *beauté* /bote/ versus *botté* /bɔte/ which arise in derived forms.)

In stressed (final) syllables, the situation is more complex. Here, we must distinguish the /e-ɛ/ pair from /ø-œ/ and /o-ɔ/. Both /e/ and /ɛ/ may occur in final open syllables, but only /ɛ/ occurs in closed position. For the round vowels, the situation is reversed. Both members of each pair occur in closed syllables,[6] but only /o/ and /ø/ occur word finally. Consider the examples in (16).

(16) OPPOSITIONS AMONG THE MID VOWELS (STRESSED POSITION)

	(a) *open syllables*	(b) *closed syllables*
e	*fée, donnerai*	—
ɛ	*fait, donnerait*	*dette, peigne*
ø	*peu, queue*	*jeûne, émeute*
œ	—	*seul, peur*
o	*haut, zéro*	*saute, rôle*
ɔ	—	*colle*

Given these constraints on the mid vowels plus the tendency of certain speakers to merge /a/ and /ɑ/ and the fact that certain dialects (those of the *Midi*) have lost any phonemic distinction between the members of these pairs, certain scholars (see Valdman 1975: 64–69) have suggested the utility of a reduced

---

6. We ignore here certain additional constraints—the absence of /ɔ/ before /z/, *rose* /roz/ but never */rɔz/, for example (in the dialect considered here). We should also note that the contrast between /ø/ and /œ/ is very rare in any case.

system for the French vowels, both for pedagogical purposes and as an indication of potential change. This system would have the structure (for the oral vowels) shown in (17):

(17)   i   ü   u
            e   ø   ə   o
                    a

In this analysis, the realizations of the pairs of mid vowels [e-ɛ], [o-œ], [ø-ɔ] would be largely determined by syllable structure according to the "loi de position." Those cases which preserve the phonemic distinction (the future versus the conditional, say) would have to be learned separately on an item-by-item basis linked to the specific grammatical function involved, reflecting the traditional principle of the avoidance of homonymy. Whether or not the SF system actually ends up in the reduced structure of (17) remains to be seen; but the concept, not to mention the attempts at prediction, are certainly interesting.

2.1.4   *Nasalized vowels*

Up to this point, we have considered that SF has the four nasalized vowels /ɛ̃ œ̃ ɔ̃ ɑ̃/. In fact, this is only partially true. There is a strong tendency, virtually complete for the younger generations of speakers, to merge /œ̃/ with /ɛ̃/ as a front unrounded vowel. For these speakers, therefore, the article *un* is pronounced /ɛ̃/, and the pairs *brun-brin, emprunte-empreinte*, etc. are homophonous: /brɛ̃/ and /ɑ̃prɛ̃t/ respectively.

Secondly, the traditional notation we have been using for the nasalized vowels is phonetically somewhat misleading, if not inaccurate. In strict phonetic terms, the front unrounded nasalized vowel is not [ɛ̃], but something closer to the more open vowel [æ̃] (comparable to the vowel in North American English *can't*). In the same way, the back rounded vowel is not [ɔ̃], but a more closed variant [õ]. The nasalized system of current SF could then be represented as in (18).

(18) SF NASALIZED VOWELS (PHONETICS)

õ

æ̃   ɑ̃

This phonetic detail will become important when we consider several modifications that have affected the Canadian dialect. There is, however, both a practical and a theoretical reason for maintaining the traditional notation of these vowels as /ɛ̃/, /ɑ̃/ and so on. This involves certain alternations between nasalized vowels and their oral counterparts, as illustrated below in (19).

(19)	ɛ̃	*vain*	ɛn	*vaine*
	ɛ̃	*américain*	ɛn	*américaine*
	ɛ̃	*sain*	ɛn	*saine*
	ɛ̃	*craint*	ɛɲ	*craignons*
	ɔ̃	*bon*	ɔn	*bonne*
	ɔ̃	*don*	ɔn	*donner*
	ɔ̃	*klaxon*	ɔn	*klaxonner*
	ɑ̃	*plan*	an	*planer*
	ɑ̃	*catalan*	an	*catalane*
	ɑ̃	*ruban*	an	*enrubanner*

Given that /ɛ̃/, /ɔ̃/ are in a consistent relationship with /ɛn/, /ɔn/, it seems reasonable to maintain a single more abstract representation for the vowel, reflecting this constant link, in spite of certain minor phonetic differences. We will return to this question in a subsequent section.

2.1.5   *Vowels and semi-vowels*

We saw earlier that, corresponding to the high vowels /i ü u/, French has three semi-vowels or glides /j ɥ w/. While it is possible to find many cases where the semi-vowels exist independently (*paille* /paj/, *truite* /trɥit/, *oui* /wi/ and so on), there are other words which sometimes contain a vowel, sometimes a semi-vowel, in the same position. Consider the items in (20).

(20)   *il scie*   /si/   —   *il sciait*   /sjɛ/
      je lie   /li/   —   *nous lions* /ljɔ̃/
      tu tues /tü/ —   *vous tuez* /tɥe/
      il sue   /sü/ —   *il suait*   /sɥɛ/
      ils louent /lu/ —   *ils louaient* /lwɛ/
      je joue /ʒu/ —   *nous jouons* /ʒwɔ̃/

We see here that when a high vowel precedes another vowel, it is converted into the corresponding semi-vowel: *jou + ons* /ʒu + ɔ̃/ → /ʒwɔ̃/ and so forth. This process is fully productive in French; each time the appropriate conditions are met, we will find an alternation between a high vowel (preceding consonants or in final position) versus a semi-vowel (preceding a vowel).

One of the conditions on this rule is particularly interesting. It is possible in SF to observe sequences such as /pj, sj, ʒw, lw, tü, sü/ and so on at the beginning of syllables, but sequences of consonant + l/r + semi-vowel are impossible. We never find *plj, *trj, *slw or, that is to say, CLG sequences, syllable-initially.[7] Thus, while we see the alternation in pairs like *scie-scier*, we never find it in the items in (21).

(21)   *plie*   /pli/   —   *plier*   /plie/
      crie   /kri/   —   *crier*   /krie/
      confluent /kɔ̃flü/ —   *confluer*   /kɔ̃flüe/
      congru /kɔ̃grü/ —   *congruence* /kɔ̃grüɑ̃s/
      troue   /tru/   —   *trouer*   /true/
      cloue   /klu/   —   *clouer*   /klue/

---

7. There are a few exceptions to this: *trois, fluide, truite* /trwa, flɥid, trɥit/ etc., but none of these, except for the sequence CLɥi as in *fluide*, plays any role in the vowel—semi-vowel alternation.

There are, in fact, occasions where the alternation prompts the insertion of /j/ between /i/ and a following vowel, as in (22).

(22) *je crie*   /kri/   — *je criais*   /krijɛ/
    je plie   /pli/   — *je pliais*   /plijɛ/

In certain cases, this additional insertion is seen in non-standard or dialectal alternates involving the deletion of schwa and the constraint against /CLj/ sequences. Consider the conditional verb forms in (23).

(23) *nous achèterions*   (a) /aʃetərjɔ̃/
                              (b) /aʃtrijɔ̃/

    vous compléteriez   (a) /kɔ̃plɛtərje/
                              (b) /kɔ̃plɛtrije/

    nous appellerions   (a) /apɛlərjɔ̃/
                              (b) /apɛlrijɔ̃/

The (a) forms are the standard pronunciations (see Warnant 1968). But if the mute-*e* is deleted in the conditional, in *appellɇrions*, for example, we find the sequence *lrj* which is not allowed by the constraint against CVG sequences: */apɛlrjɔ̃/. In this type of case, the orthographic *i* of the conditional remains /i/, giving rise to the sequence /apɛlriɔ̃/, which then requires the insertion of /j/: /apɛlrijɔ̃/. This particularly complex interaction of general constraints, phonological alternations and stylistic or dialectal factors illustrates the type of problem we will encounter in the consideration of the CF material to follow.

2.1.6   *Stress and syllabification*

It is a commonplace to observe that in SF the final syllable of the word is stressed, unless it contains a schwa, in which case the penultimate syllable bears the accent. Given the great frequency of deletion of final schwa in colloquial French, the words of (24) would be accented as indicated (primary stress is indicated by the diacritic mark ´ over the vowel):

(24) américaine /amerikén/
Canada /kanadá/
craignons /krɛɲɔ̃́/
fête /fɛ́t(ə)/
joli /ʒɔlí/
klaxon /klaksɔ̃́/
partir /partír/
photographie /fotografí/
porte /pɔ̃́rt(ə)/
presque /prɛ́sk(ə)/

On occasion, it is possible to find the pronoun *le* in final position (in imperative constructions), in which case we might claim that schwa can bear the stress. But when this happens, we find that the final vowel in these structures has invariably merged with /ø/ or /œ/, so that the generalization that schwa is never stressed can be maintained: *faites-le*, in other words, is pronounced /fɛtlǿ/.

This generalization regarding stress placement applies only to words cited in isolation. When words are combined into phrases, however, there is suppression of all but the final primary stress. As a result, there is but a single group stress, again on the final syllable of the phonological group, as in (25) (` indicates a reduced stress).

(25) prèsque finí
pòrte fermée
jolìe maisón
photographìe intéressánte
partìr avec mes amís

Standard dialects of SF accentuate the final syllables of words and phrases. There are, however, two ways in which non-final accents may arise. The first is through the use of the so-called "accent d'insistance", which reinforces the first syllable of words, often through supportive or additional doubling of the consonant of that syllable, as in (26).

(26)   *c'est terrible*   /sɛttériblə/
       impossible   /ɛ̃ppɔ̃siblə/
       quel crétin   /kɛlkkrétɛ̃/
       intolérable   /ɛ̃ttɔlerablə/

The links of the "accent d'insistance" to emotional or excited speech are indicated by the nature of the examples, although there is also a tendency to extend the use of this type of speech style beyond its original limits.

This tendency is reinforced by a second type of non-final stress: the use of initial or penultimate stress in colloquial speech. Examples of this phenomenon are found in (27), taken from the work of Fonagy 1979. (The italics indicate a non-final accented syllable within the phonological phrase.)

(27)   *Non-final stress*

six lap*in*s	≠	s'*il* a peint
ces *eaux* monotones	≠	*ces* eaux monotones
une *nou*velle période	≠	une nou*velle* période
une statue *co*lossale	≠	une statue coloss*ale*
la *deu*xième année française		
*do*ssier		
*mo*notone		
une *pen*sée fatale		
un *procès* verbal		
la *plus* aveugle passion		

On the basis of the studies in Léon and Fonagy 1979, plus the historical material contained therein, we may conclude that non-final stress is relatively frequent in French. When the links between vowel length and stress are considered below, we will be able to see the implications of this analysis for the CF material.

The phonological subordination of the word within the group is reflected not just in stress assignment, but also in the behaviour of schwa, in elision and in liaison. Several aspects of the deletion of schwa, for example, are defined with respect to the boundaries of phonological phrases, themselves reflecting major syntactic phrases, and liaison takes place within such phrases but not between them. The role of the phonological phrase is also evident in the last phenomenon to be discussed—the tendency of SF toward open syllables. Given any sequence VCV within a phrase, for example, SF will normally syllabify it as V$CV. In addition, the syllabification in VCCV sequences will be consistently V$CCV if the two consonants are normally permitted in syllable-initial position. This tendency is seen in the words in (28).

(28) | *V$CV* | *V$CCV* | *VC$CV* |
| --- | --- | --- |
| *demain* | *peuplier* | *partir* |
| /də-mɛ̃/ | /pø-pli-e/ | /par-tir/ |
| *infini* | *constant* | *actif* |
| /ɛ̃-fi-ni/ | /kɔ̃-stɑ̃/ | /ak-tif/ |
| *photographie* | *patrie* | *artiste* |
| /fo-to-gra-fi/ | /pa-tri/ | /ar-tist/ |
| *canadien* | *décret* | *caneton* |
| /ka-na-djɛ̃/ | /de-krɛ/ | /kan-tɔ̃/ |

The tendency is valid not just word-internally, but also between words in groups, leading to the phenomenon generally called "enchaînement", illustrated in (29).

(29)   *les États-Unis*   /le-ze-ta-zü-ni/
       ma petite amie   /ma-pə-ti-ta-mi/
       vous êtes actif   /vu-zɛt-zak-tif/

The process is pushed to the exteme in such examples as /galamɑ̃dəlarɛnalaturmaɲanim/ which, if intonation, pauses and other relevant details are (artificially) ignored, may represent among others the two sentences, "*Gal, amant de la reine, alla, tour magnanime,*" and "*galament de l'arène à la tour Magne, à Nîmes.*" With these examples, we conclude our brief summary of the vowel system of SF, and now turn to the consonants.

2.2   *The consonant phonemes of SF*

The SF consonant inventory is given in (30) and illustrated in (31).

(30)   SF CONSONANTS

	labial	apical	(alveo) palatal	velar	uvular
stops	p	t		k	
	b	d		g	
fricatives	f	s	ʃ		
	v	z	ʒ		
nasals	m	n	ɲ		
liquids		l			R

In contradistinction to the SF vowels, the consonant inventory is relatively simple and without major idiosyncracy. The consonants are divided into four main types—stops, fricatives, nasals and liquids—and distributed throughout the four major places of articulation (plus the uvular trill or fricative /R/). The occurrence of each consonant in the major contexts within the word is exemplified below in (31).

(31) EXAMPLES OF SF CONSONANTS IN VARIOUS CONTEXTS

	# __ V	V __ V	__ #
p	père	couper	coupe
b	banc	rabais	robe
t	tout	ôter	toute
d	dent	vider	vide
k	coup	bloquer	sec
g	gant	blaguer	bague
f	fort	effort	soif
v	vert	sauver	chauve
s	cire	presser	grosse
z	zéro	arroser	rose
ʃ	chemin	sécher	mèche
ʒ	général	bougie	rouge
m	mère	blâmer	crème
n	nous	sonner	reine
ɲ	__*	dédaigner	peigne
l	loup	coller	pile
R	rare	pari	corps

---

* Except in loan words, slang or child language, /ɲ/ does not appear word-initially in SF: *gnocchi, gnaf-gnaf, niaiseux, gnognon,* etc. (*niais, nier* and so on are phonemically /nj/).

2.2.1 *Consonant allophones*

As we did with the vowels, we will now review some of the major phonetic properties of SF consonants, concentrating on those aspects that will be of use in subsequent discussion of CF. To begin with, we should note that the SF apical consonants /t, d, s, z, n, l/ are apico-dental, produced with tongue contact against the upper teeth, rather than apico-alveolar like their English counterparts. The /l/, in addition, has no velar allophone, being realized in all contexts as a "light" *l* (see section 2.0).[8] The phonetic contrast may be seen in such pairs as French *Alpes, altitude* versus English *help, altitude*. Finally, we should note that the English voiceless stops are aspirated in various positions—obligatorily in the contexts # __; V __ V́, and optionally in word-final position: *pin, tin, kin, upon, attain, nip, pit, kick,* etc. SF consonants, on the other hand, are never aspirated, as can be established by comparing French *peine, tout, coup* with English *pen, two, coo* and so on.

2.2.2 *Varying realizations of /R/*

SF has a single "r"-phoneme, normally realized as a uvular fricative, occasionally as a trill [R] (compare also the German *r* in *raus, rauchen* etc.). Given the variety of "r"-sounds in language in general, it is not surprising to find that, even in continental France, there exist differing regional or social pronunciations. Two of the most common are the apical trill (which we will represent as [r̃] as in Spanish *roja* or *perro*) and the so-called flap (represented as [ř] as in Spanish *pero*). Both of the latter can be heard in songs or on the stage, for example, as well as regionally. It goes without saying that these differences will be important in the CF context, as will various other SF features in the material to follow.

2.2.3 *Devoicing and voicing assimilation*

All the sonorant consonants of French—the nasals, liquids and glides (semi-vowels)—have two allophones determined by the voicing of the preceding segment. Normally, the sonorants will be voiced. When a voiceless obstruent (stop or fricative) precedes these sonorants, however, they become voiceless by assimilation to

---

8. Historically speaking, however, there was a "dark" or velarized *l* in Early Old French. This segment became fully velarized and converted to /w/, which formed a diphthong with the preceding vowel, and was written as *u*. Compare *altitude - haut, cheval - chevaux, cheveu - chevelure, bateau - batelier* and so on.

the preceding voiceless segment, as the examples in (32) make clear.[9] (Subscript ₀ indicates a devoiced consonant.)

(32)   C __ V   C __ #

        plan   [pl̥ɑ̃]   peuple   [pœpl̥]
        prends   [pr̥ɑ̃]   battre   [batr̥]
        la semaine [lasm̥en]   rythme   [ritm̥]
        pneu   [pn̥ø]   __*
        pied   [pj̥e]   __
        puits   [pɥ̥i]   __
        poids   [pw̥ɑ]   __

---

* SF does not permit final sequences of /pn pj pɥ pw/, nor does it in general permit /Cɲ/ clusters, with the exception of /rɲ/ as in *epargner*).

These forms, where sonorants devoice in contact with preceding voiceless obstruents, exemplify one major type of voicing assimilation in SF. There is a second, which affects clusters of obstruents either word-internally or at word boundaries. In this case, the first, i.e. the syllable-final consonant, which is in weak position, takes on the voicing of the second or syllable-initial segment. (Recall that VCCV sequences are syllabified as VC$CV in most cases, and that voiced obstruents differ from voiceless obstruents in at least two phonetic features: voicing and tenseness versus laxness or *fortis* versus *lenis*. Thus, [p] is voiceless and tense, [b] voiced and lax. As a consequence, [b̥] represents a voiceless lax bilabial stop, while [p̬] signals a voiced but tense stop. Both [b̥] and [p̬] remain distinct from [p] and [b] respectively through phonetic differences of tenseness. The same applies, of course, to other obstruents). These differences are illustrated in (33).

---

9. We ignore certain examples of devoicing after voiced obstruents in final position: *sabre* [sabr̥], *sable* [sabl̥] and so on. (See Malmberg 1969:134.)

(33) ASSIMILATION IN OBSTRUENT CLUSTERS

(a)   *voiced*   *voiceless*

	voiced		voiceless
ro*b*e *ch*ic	bʃ		b̥ʃ
va*g*ue *s*entiment	gs	→	g̥s
beaucoup *d*e *ch*oses	dʃ		d̥ʃ
ro*s*e *t*raditionnel	zt		z̥t

(b)   *voiceless*   *voiced*

	voiceless		voiced
cou*p*e *d*e vinaigre	pd		p̬d
ce*tt*e *d*ent	td		t̬d
be*c d*e gaz	kd	→	k̬d
va*ch*e *b*ête	ʃb		ʃ̬b
fau*ss*e *d*ent	sd		s̬d

(̬ indicates voicing of normally voiceless C)

Finally, in syllable-initial clusters of obstruents (unlike the obstruent-sonorant clusters of (32)), we must recognize a third type of assimilation, conditioned by the difference between strong (= voiceless) and weak (= voiced) obstruents. In this case, the weak segment assimilates to the strong, regardless of their relative position. Thus, in *je sais*, weak /ʒ/ precedes strong /s/ while in *cheval*, weak /v/ follows strong /ʃ/. The weak consonant becomes voiceless in both cases, as in the rest of the examples in (34).

(34) SYLLABLE INITIAL OBSTRUENT CLUSTERS ($CC)

*je s*ais	ʒs		ʃs	(→ ʃ)
*je f*ais	ʒf		ʃf	
*je p*ars	ʒp	→	ʃp	
*ch*e*v*al	ʃv		ʃf	
*ch*e*v*ille	ʃv		ʃf	
*s*e*m*aine	sm		sm̥	

In general, then, we see that SF belongs to that widespread class of languages where consonant clusters (in which at least the first member is an obstruent) tend to agree in voicing, both within words and at the junctions between words. Both obstruents and sonorants, therefore, have two allophones, a voiced and voiceless, depending on phonological context.

2.2.4   *Gaps in the consonant inventory*

In terms of the set of phonemes in the SF consonant inventory, and in terms of the phonemic composition of words, we often find that the most interesting problems are involved in the presence or absence of whole phonemes, rather than in the varying allophones of a particular phoneme depending on context. A brief examination of (30), therefore, reveals the absence of any affricates. (Compare English /č ǰ/ '*church, judge,*' Spanish /č/ '*chico, macho,*' German /p^f t^s/ '*Pferd, zahlen,*' and so on.) This is not to say that affricate-like segments do not occur in SF. They may be found phonetically in *tas de choses, cette chemise, pas de jury*, for example, but in each of these cases they may be analyzed as a sequence of /t + ʃ/ /d + ʒ/, etc., and not as a phonological affricate (unlike certain CF segments).

Another type of segment absent from the phonological inventory of SF is the velar nasal /ŋ/. This gap results in an incomplete series of nasals in the four principal orders: labial, apical, palatal, velar. But in fact, it is somewhat inaccurate to speak of the complete absence of /ŋ/, since this gap is being filled in SF in two ways. We may first cite a large number of English loans in *-ing*, which have the effect of bringing in a large number of occurrences of /ŋ/ (the latter four particularly popular as emblems on track suits):

(35)   *pouding*
       parking
       smoking
       footing
       crossing
       training
       jogging

SURVEY OF STANDARD FRENCH PHONOLOGY 37

As we will see later, the influence of loan words may be considerable in filling gaps in phonemic inventories, or even in modifying the structural properties of phonological systems.

2.2.5   *Modifications involving nasals*

The second way in which /ŋ/ is being introduced into SF is through a broader process of nasalization of oral consonants in nasal contexts. It is not uncommon to hear /b d g/ realized as /m n ŋ/ when the stops are adjacent to nasals. Consider the forms in (36).

(36)   a*dm*irer   [anmirer]
       une lo*ngue m*inute   [ünlɔ̃ŋminüt]
       dia*gno*stique   [djaŋnɔstik]
       la gra*nde d*ame   [lagrɑ̃ndam]
       ça to*mbe m*al   [satɔ̃mmal]
       il est complètement din*gue m*on ami   [... dɛ̃ŋmɔnami]
       la bo*mb*e   [labɔm]

As a result of this process, we see nasal /ŋ/ making an appearance through the operation of internal phonological processes, in addition to its role in loanwords.

The further type of change involving nasals in SF affects the relation between the palatal nasal /ɲ/ and the sequence /n+j/. There is an interesting process at work whereby /ɲ/ has a tendency to be realized as /nj/, merging with original /nj/. We see the effects of this phenomenon in such forms as:

(37)   *panier*   [panje]
       union   [ünjɔ̃]

              versus

       baigner   [bɛnje]   <   /bɛɲe/
       accompagner   [akɔ̃panje]   <   /akɔ̃paɲe/
       brugnon   [brünjɔ̃]   <   /brüɲɔ̃/

There are also sporadic instances of the passage of /n+j/ to /ɲ/, as in *manière* [maɲɛr], *miniature* [miɲatür], further attesting to the confusion between the two pronunciations. Malmberg 1969:107 interprets the change /ɲ/ → /n+j/ between vowels as the re-analysis of the single segment /ɲ/ as /n+j/, so that phonemically *baigner* is now /bɛnje/, *peignons*, /pɛnjɔ̃/ and so on. If this is correct, the phoneme /ɲ/ is perhaps in the initial stages disappearing from SF, being replaced by /n+j/.[10] An additional process affects the palatal nasal in Canadian French, as we will see below.

2.2.6   *Aspirate* -h

Every speaker (or learner) of French knows that there are two types of orthographic "*h*-words" in SF. Some, like *homme*, *heure*, *heureuse*, behave phonologically exactly as if the words began with vowels; the *h* is ignored. Such words are indistinguishable from *ombre*, *oeuvre*, *européen* in their phonological behaviour. Other forms, those with "*h*-aspiré" and which constitute the irregular class, behave in various ways as if they began with a consonant, even though phonetically they are also vowel-initial. This behaviour is demonstrated by the processes of elision, liaison, the selection of certain irregular determiners and adjectives, and the violation of sequential constraints on phonemes. Consider the forms in (38).

(38)   COMPARISON OF "H-ASPIRÉ" WORDS WITH CONSONANT AND VOWEL-INITIAL WORDS

(a)	#C	(b)	#V
le garçon	/ləgarsɔ̃/	*l'arc*	/lark/
la fille	/lafij/	*l'amie*	/lami/
ce garçon	/səgarsɔ̃/	*cet arc*	/sɛtark/
ces garçons	/segarsɔ̃/	*ces arcs*	/sezark/
un vieux garçon	/œ̃vjø garsɔ̃/	*un vieil arc*	/œ̃vjɛjark/

---

10. A similar process is affecting /l + j/, which in rapid speech may simplify to /j/: *soulier* /suje/, *filière* /fijer/, *collier* /kɔje/ and so on.

(c)	# "*h-aspiré*"	(d)	# "*h-non-aspiré*"
le héros	/lǝero/	*l'homme*	/lɔm/
la hache	/laaʃ/	*l'heure*	/lœr/
ce héros	/sǝero/	*cet homme*	/sɛtɔm/
ces héros	/seero/	*ces hommes*	/sezɔm/
un vieux héros	/œ̃vjøero/	*un vieil homme*	/œ̃vjɛjɔm/

In (38c), the "*h*-aspiré" words do not undergo elision of *le* or *la*, require *ce* rather than *cet*, do not permit liaison, and require the form of *vieux* found before consonants. They behave, in other words, just like the forms of (38a), which begin with a consonant. The "non-aspirate-*h*" words of (38d) show the patterns of vowel-initial words in (38b). There are, in addition, constraints on sequences of phonemes in SF that prohibit schwa from preceding a vowel within words, and also prohibit nasalized vowels before other vowels: *ǝV, *ṼV. Again, "aspirate-*h*" permits the violation of these constraints: *rehausser* /rǝose/ *dehors* /dǝor/, *enhardir* /ãardir/, *Panhard* /pãar/ etc. "Aspirate-*h*" words, as we can again see by comparing (38a-c) with (38b-d), behave as if they were consonant-initial,[11] in spite of the fact they begin with a vowel.

One can hear the sound [h] in SF, as an emphatic, interjected sound. We also find glottal stop occurring between vowels. In fact, the *Robert* dictionary uses ['] (glottal stop) as a symbol to indicate "*h*-aspiré" words. The problem with this approach is that neither [h] nor ['] occurs consistently with such words. Depending on style or on context, either of these sounds may occur word-initially or as a hiatus breaker where there is no "*h*-aspiré" involved. There is no consistent connection between *h* and [h] or [']; attempts to use either of these as a phonetic correlate of *h* are seriously deficient.

To conclude this section, we may note that, in terms of the properties of (38), "*h*-aspiré" words are irregular. Their phonetic properties are contradictory to the behaviour they condition in the

---

11. At the time that the behaviour in (38) was determined, the great majority of these words did begin with an articulated consonant [h], present in the Germanic source of these loans. This [h] subsequently dropped, but only after the irregular behaviour of the preceding words was established.

words preceding them. The irregularity of the "*h*-aspiré" words is manifested in a number of ways. First, authorities do not agree on the list of words that belong to the class, and there is a constant tendency to regularize these words by placing them in the class (38d): *les haricots* /lezariko/, for example. Moreover, there is a tendency for derived or related forms to have a "non-aspirate-*h*" and to pattern with the forms in (38d), even if the root contains the "aspirate": *le héros*, but *l'héroine, l'héroisme*; *le hérald* but *l'héraldiste, héraldique* and so on. In retrospect, therefore, we see that "aspirate-*h*" has little to do with [h]; we are dealing rather with a morphological and lexical than with a phonological question.

2.2.7   *Final consonants*

The preceding section dealt with phenomena at the beginning of a sub-class of words. There are also questions to be discussed relating to the behaviour of consonants in word-final position. First, there is a strong tendency in informal speech to simplify final clusters of obstruent plus liquid by deleting the liquid (subsequent to the dropping of word-final schwa) when the cluster to be simplified either precedes a consonant or is in sentence-final position. Consider the items in (39).

(39)   DELETION OF WORD-FINAL LIQUIDS

j'en ai quatre	/kat/
le couple	/kup/
il siffle	/sif/
un joli arbre	/arb/
quatre maisons	/katmezõ/
table de nuit	/tabdənɥi/
le prêtre vient	/ləprɛtvjẽ/

The second problem is the converse of the first—the tendency to pronounce certain final consonants which are normally silent. On occasion, there is semantic specialization involved; the two forms taking on different meanings. Consider the items in (40), where the frequency of pronunciations with the final consonant is increasing.

(40)
tous	/tu/—/tus/
plus	/plü/—/plüs/
but	/büt/
fait	/fɛt/
août	/ut/
ananas	/ananas/
moeurs	/mœrs/
soit	/swat/
tandis que	/tãdiskə/

(In this last case, the influence of *lorsque, puisque*, and no doubt *parce que*, is evident.)

The concluding problem we will discuss in connection with final consonants is that of liaison. It is well known that many SF words present two forms, a long one containing a final consonant and a short one without that consonant. For this liaison consonant two conditions are necessary: the words in question must be in close syntactic link (pronoun plus verb, article or adjective plus noun, and so on) and the second word, to which liaison is made, must begin with a vowel. Consider the forms of (41).

(41)
nous/venons	nous‿arrivons
elle/a	elles‿ont
les/filles	les‿amies
petit/garçon	petit‿ami
petits/garçons	petits‿amis
trop/grand	trop‿aimable
grand/garçon	grand‿homme

It is traditional to recognize three types of liaison: obligatory (as between pronoun and verb, singular adjective plus noun), prohibited (across phonological phrase boundaries, with certain words such as *et*, or various adverbs, etc.) and optional (modal plus infinitive, plural noun plus adjective, and so on). The latter, of course, are subject to stylistic variation, with the incidence of liaison being reduced as the level progresses from formal to informal. In (42), for example, we would not expect to find liaison in informal speech:

(42) *je vais y aller*   /ʒvɛiale/
     je suis en colère   /ʃɥiãkɔlɛr/
     il faut aller   /ifoale/
     des enfants aimables   /dezãfãɛmabl/

In addition to the reduction of liaison in informal speech, we find an opposite tendency. Very often, the liaison consonant occurs in the plural, realized as /z/. It also happens, then, that in certain semantically plural contexts, we will find an inserted /z/, even though the grammatical context does not call for one. We will also on occasion find /z/ (less often /t/) as a simple hiatus breaker, independently of any semantic motivation. Consider the false liaisons in (43):

(43) *quatre enfants*   /katzãfã/
     vingts hommes   /vɛ̃zɔm/
     donne-moi-z-en   /dɔnmwazã/
     sous une forme ou-z une autre /suzünfɔrmuzünotr/
     elle n'est pas venu-z encore   /... vənüzãkɔr/
     qu'on-z y tient   /kɔ̃zitjɛ̃/
     ils arrivaient-z à les enlever /... arivɛza.../

This concludes our brief survey of the phonology of SF. In addition to the basic structures, we have concentrated here on two general domains: those properties which appear in colloquial speech, and those aspects which will help to illuminate the CF material to follow. We now turn, therefore, to the phonology of Canadian French.

Further Reading—Standard French Phonology

There exist a number of basic reference manuals dealing with the phonology of Standard French. Among these are:
> Fouché (1959)
> Malmberg (1969)
> Martinet (1945)
> Walter (1976)
> Walter (1977a)

Colloquial French is dealt with in:
> Bauche (1920)
> Frei (1929)
> Guiraud (1965)
> Morin (1979)
> Rigeault (ed.) (1971)

More technical but still general discussion, linked to current theoretical debates, occurs in:
> Dell (1980)
> Schane (1968)
> Tranel (1981a)

There is a wealth of treatments of the historical development of the French language. Three basic manuals are:
> Nyrop (1930)
> Pope (1934)
> Price (1971)

Finally, dictionaries of pronunciation provide much useful data. Among the most respected are:
> Lerond (1980)
> Martinet and Walter (1973)
> Warnant (1968)

CHAPTER 3

The Vowel System of Canadian French

3.0 *Introduction*

In this chapter we will survey the structure of the CF vowel system, a system which on the abstract level is similar to that of SF. However, when questions of the realization of this system, of the concrete phonetic properties of the North American variety, are considered, we will be struck by a number of marked differences of substance. This fascinating divergence contains much material of theoretical as well as descriptive relevance, and we will have occasion to return to certain theoretical matters in later chapters. For the moment, however, let us view the CF vowel system against the background of the SF model outlined in the previous chapter.

3.1 *Vowel length*

Recall that in SF, long vowels are restricted to closed stressed syllables,[1] and are of two main types: (a) the intrinsically long vowels /ø o ɑ/ plus nasalized vowels; (b) vowels lengthened by the consonants /v z ʒ r/. There also exist a very few representatives of an /ɛ/—/ɛ:/ opposition, but the opposition is variable and has all but disappeared from current use. These SF long vowels are illustrated again in (1).

(1) LONG VOWELS IN SF

    (a) *intrinsically long* (/ø o ɑ/, Ṽ)

ancre	[ɑ̃:kr]
honte	[ɔ̃:t]
jeûne	[ʒø:n]
le nôtre	[ləno:t]
pâte	[pɑ:t]
saute	[so:t]

---

1. We exclude, at least for the moment, consideration of the "accent d'insistance" or "accent affectif", which is stylistically marked, albeit rather frequent in colloquial speech. (In this regard consult Seguinot (ed.) 1976.)

(b) lengthened by a "consonne allongeante"

épave	[epaːv]
peur	[pœːr]
juge	[ʒüːʒ]
port	[pɔːr]
prise	[priːz]
pur	[püːr]
rêve	[rɛːv]
toge	[tɔːʒ]

(c) the /ɛ/ - /ɛː/ opposition

belle	/bɛl/	bêle	/bɛːl/
bette	/bɛt/	bête	/bɛːt/
faite	/fɛt/	fête	/fɛːt/
lettre	/lɛtr/	l'être	/lɛːtr/
mettre	/mɛtr/	maître	/mɛːtr/

(In (1), we have not included the pair [a - ɑː] (*patte* - *pâte* and so on) as reflecting a *phonemic* distinction of vowel length, even if [ɑː] is often long. The difference, in phonemic terms, is one of quality—front versus back—rather than length: /a/-/ɑ/, not /a/-/aː/. One strong argument for this interpretation is found in the behaviour of these vowels in final open syllables, where both segments are short, but where the quality difference remains: *la - là* [la - lɑ]; *ma - mât* [ma - mɑ], never *[laː], [mɑː], etc.) In general terms, when CF is compared to SF, the former is characterized in part by the much greater importance it attributes to differences of vowel length. On the one hand, the /ɛ/-/ɛː/ opposition is stable if not expanding in CF, unlike SF, where it has all but disappeared. On the other, we find a much greater presence of pretonic vowel length. In what follows, we will also discuss several phenomena in CF which serve to reinforce the distinction between long and short vowels, thereby highlighting those syllables which do contain long segments. First, however, consider several examples of long /ɛ:/ in CF. Even in the absence of minimal pairs, these vowels remain long and invariant in Canadian speech. The vowel /ɛ:/ is illustrated in (2) (see also Santerre 1974:137-138).

(2)   /ɛ:/ in CF

>   *aide*   *freine*
>   *arrête*   *guêpe*
>   *baisse*   *honnête*
>   *bête*   *Lefebvre*
>   *embête*   *maître (≠ mettre)*
>   *enquête*   *mêle*
>   *épaisse*   *même*
>   *évêque*   *problème*
>   *fenêtre*   *rêve (≠ lève/ɛ/)*
>   *fête (≠ faite)*   *tête*
>   *fève*   *traître*
>   *fraîche*

We may next turn to pretonic long vowels in CF, i.e. to long vowels in non-final syllables. These are exemplified in the left-hand column of (3), with related words given to the right.

(3)   PRETONIC LONG VOWELS IN CF

>   *arrêter*   [arɛ:te]   *arrêt*   [arɛ]
>   *câlice*   [kɔ:lIs]
>   *deux cents* [dø:sã]
>   *du bon sens* [d^{Z}übõ:sã]
>   *écoeurer*   [ekœ:re]   *coeur*   [kœ:r]
>   *fêter*   [fɛ:te]   *fête*   [fɛ:t]
>   *grêler*   [grɛ:le]   *grêle*   [grɛ:l]
>   *heureux*   [ø:rø]

il est faché	[jefɑːʃe]		
je comprends	[kɔ̃ːprɑ̃]		
lâcher	[lɑːʃe]	*lâche*	[lɑːʃ]
maîtrise	[mɛːtriːz]	*maître*	[mɛːtr]
neiger	[neːʒe]	*neige*	[neːʒ]
niaiseux	[njɛːzø]		
prêtresse	[prɛːtrɛs]	*prêtre*	[prɛːtr]
rêverie	[rɛːvri]	*rêve*	[rɛːv]
sâbler	[sɑːble]	*sable*	[sɑːbl]
se pâmer	[spɑːme]		
terrain	[tɛːrɛ̃]	*terre*	[tɛːr]

In general terms, there are two main types of pretonic long vowels in CF. The first type reflects the long vowels we have already seen in the discussion of SF (cf. (1) above): intrinsically long vowels or vowels lengthened by a *consonne allongeante*. Such long vowels may occur in a word that is itself part of a more complex word. In such a case, the vowels remain long, but are followed by a suffix and consequently occur in non-final (pretonic) position. Thus, the vowels of *sable* and *pire* are both long, the first intrinsically, the second lengthened by /r/. When suffixes are added to these words (*sableuse, rempirer*) the /a/ and /i/ remain long, even though they are no longer in the final syllable of the complex words. Further examples of this first type of pretonic long vowels are found in (4).

(4) LONG VOWELS IN THE ROOTS OF COMPLEX WORDS

    (a) *intrinsically long vowels*

sable	sablé	sableuse	sablonneux	sabler
passe	passé	passant		
lâche	lâcher			
honte	honteux			

(b) *vowels lengthened by lengthening consonants*

rêve	rêver	rêverie	rêveur
pire	rempirer		
juge	jugement		
rive	rivière		
bave	baver	bavure	
beurre	beurrer	beurrée	
dore	dorer	doré	dorure

Secondly, any of the intrinsically long vowels of (1a) above, as well as /e/,[2] may also occur long in pretonic syllables, independently of the morphological structure of the words in question. This phenomenon occurs most frequently when the vowels are in open syllables. Thus, in a word like *comprends*, the /ɔ̃/ is an intrinsically long vowel in an open, pretonic syllable, and may be lengthened in CF: [kɔ̃:prã]. Further examples of this type of long vowel, including the vowel of articles that are closely linked to the following noun, are found in (5).

(5)
	maison	e:
	braker	e:
	des oeufs	e:
	feutré	ø:
	jeûner	ø:
	jeudi	ø:

---

2. Presumably, /e/ could also be considered extrinsically long, parallel to the other higher-mid vowels /ø/ and /o/. Unlike SF, where /e/ is excluded from closed syllables and hence from lengthening, it occurs in closed position in CF and consequently lengthens like the other vowels under discussion.

côté	oː
chômage	oː
saucer	oː
santé	ãː
le pr*in*temps	ɛ̃ː
*in*struit	ɛ̃ː
h*um*blement	œ̃ː
un gars	œ̃ː
m*on*diale	ɔ̃ː
je c*om*prends	ɔ̃ː
ça a bien du b*on* sens	ɔ̃ː
m*on* gars	ɔ̃ː

In general, pretonic lengthening in CF, while optional and variable, is considerably more extensive than in SF: in CF, all tense vowels may potentially lengthen in pretonic open syllables.

Finally, we should note that there are several long vowels arising through the fusion of vowel sequences that occur in morphologically or syntactically complex constructions. Vowel length thus contrasts in examples such as those of (6).

(6) *il est après faire*   /jetaprɛfajr/
     il était après faire   /jetaːprɛfajr/   (< aa)
     vous êtes malade   /vzɛtmalad/
     vous allez être malade /vzɛːtmalad/   (< eɛ)
     sa table   /satab/
     sur la table   /saːtab/

We will briefly discuss such cases in the final chapter.

It is neither possible nor necessary to go into complete detail regarding the formal properties of the description of the lengthening processes we have discussed in this section. Nevertheless, because formal descriptions render explicit the nature and the inter-relationships of the phenomena, and because they often serve as convenient shorthand indications, we will present below initial formulations of the rules in question. (These formulae make use of the notational conventions discussed under *Notation and Abbreviations* in the prefatory material.)

(7) VOWEL LENGTHENING

(a) *Intrinsically long vowels (obligatory)*

$$\begin{bmatrix} V \\ -\text{high} \\ +\text{tense} \\ +\text{nasal} \end{bmatrix} \rightarrow [+\text{long}] \ / \_\_ C_1 \#$$

All higher mid and nasal vowels are long in final closed syllables (see (1a)).

(b) *Lengthening consonants (obligatory)*

$$V \rightarrow [+\text{long}] \ / \_\_ \begin{bmatrix} C \\ +\text{cont} \\ +\text{voice} \end{bmatrix} \#$$

In final syllables, all vowels are long preceding voiced continuants (see (1b)).

(c) *Pretonic lengthening (optional)*

$$\begin{bmatrix} V \\ \{+\text{tense}\} \\ \{+\text{nasal}\} \end{bmatrix} \rightarrow [+\text{long}] \ / \_\_ \$ C_0 \ V \ X \#$$

Higher-mid or nasal vowels may be lengthened in pretonic open syllables (see (5)).

(There is no need to write a separate rule for the vowels of (4a-b) above, assuming that rules (7a-b) lengthen these vowels in simple words and that these long vowels are carried over when suffixation occurs.)

Two obvious comments regarding distinctive feature theory are derivable on the basis of (7a–c). First, note that the tense vowels of CF presumably include the high vowels, the higher-mid vowels and /ɑ/ (at least in abstract senses of the term "tense"), but exclude /ɛ œ ɔ a ə/. This implies that the high vowels should also lengthen pretonically, and a number of them do, at least sporadically: *pourri, bureau*, etc. with [iː] and [üː]. But does the feature [tense] adequately characterize the difference between higher-mid and lower-mid vowels in CF, as well as between /a/ and /ɑ/? And what is the link between tension and nasality that would serve to provoke parallel behaviour with respect to lengthening? Perhaps nasalized vowels are also tense, and (7a, c) may simply be stated as [+tense] → [+long] in the relevant contexts. In connection with (7b), we may ask whether the conjunction of features [+continuant, +voice] adequately groups together /v z ʒ r/ in French. Concerning /v z ʒ/, there is no difficulty: they are the only voiced fricatives in French. As for /r/, it is also voiced and continuant, but its inclusion is not obvious when /l/ is excluded, for example. We are not in a position to resolve these questions, but the CF data do provide interesting material (not to say problems) for future investigations in this area of distinctive feature theory. In any case, the material from section 3.1, as well as data to occur below, motivates the following specification of CF segments (both allophones and phonemes) in terms of distinctive features. This table in (8) should be compared with the one given in (5) of Chapter 2, section 2.1 above. The table in (8) will supply the distinctive feature matrices for the discussions of CF phonology to follow.

(8) DISTINCTIVE FEATURE COMPOSITION OF CF VOWELS
     AND SEMI-VOWELS

	i ü u	I Ü U	e ø o	ɛ œ ə ɔ	a ɑ	ẽ œ̃ ɑ̃ ɔ̃	j ɥ w
syllabic	+ + +	+ + +	+ + +	+ + + +	+ +	+ + + +	- - -
high	+ + +	+ + +	+ + +	- - - -	- -	- - - -	+ + +
mid	- - -	- - -	+ + +	+ + + +	- -	+ + - +	- - -
back	- - +	- - +	- - +	- - + +	- +	- - + +	- - +
round	- + +	- + +	- + +	- + - +	- -	- + - +	- + +
tense	+ + +	- - -	+ + +	- - - -	- +	+ + + +	+ + +
nasal	- - -	- - -	- - -	- - - -	- -	+ + + +	- - -

Notes

(a) The feature [tense] plays a role here which is different from its role in SF in (5) of Chapter 2. Here, [-tense] serves to distinguish the two series of allophones of the high vowels. In addition, it distinguishes the higher-mid vowels and /ɑ/ as [+tense] from the lower-mid vowels and /a/ as [-tense].

(b) The nasal vowels are specified as [+tense], along with /e ø o ɑ/, because they are intrinsically long, and pattern phonologically with the other tense vowels.

(c) Schwa must be distinguished from each of /ɛ œ ɔ a/. Among the lower-mid vowels, the only available "slot" is to specify schwa as [+back, -round], which has some phonetic justification (see Picard 1981). In any case, the phonetic value of schwa can vary widely within the CF area.

3.2 *Vowel laxing*

Laxing in CF is a counterpart, to a certain extent, to vowel lengthening. Non-lengthened high vowels are laxed in closed final syllables and in certain pretonic contexts, and the difference between the two major realizations of each vowel phoneme, long versus short or strong versus weak, is consequently emphasized. Consider first the lax vowels in (9).

(9) I   Ü   U

   pipe   jupe   coupe
   vite   butte   croûte
   électrique   tuque   bouc
   libre   tube   j'adoube
   vide   rude   soude
   ligue   fugue   joug
   vif   bufle   touffe
   vice   juste   pousse
   riche   ruche   touche
   rime   plume   boum
   racine   lune   pitoune
   signe   —   —
   ville   nul   foule
   fille   —   grenouille (tense
                             [u] may also occur
                             before [j] for
                             certain speakers)

Note the phonetic contrast between *pipe* [pIp] and *pige* [pi:ʒ], *coupe* [kUp] and *court* [ku:r], for example. The high vowels thus have two series of allophones: short and lax versus long, tense and often diphthongized.

If we consider the vocalic inventory of CF (see the table in (10)), we can see a reason for the limitation of the laxing process to high vowels. Vowels other than the high vowels /i ü u/ are either excluded from syllables closed by many of the non-lengthening consonants, and thus do not occur in contexts provoking laxing, or they are already in opposition to a lax (or apparently lax) counterpart: /ø/ versus /œ/ (*jeûne - jeune*) and /o/ versus /ɔ/ (*saute - sotte*). Laxing of /ø/ or /o/ in this latter case would lead to the merger of the forms in question. The same applies to /a/ versus /ɑ/ (*patte - pâte*). Furthermore, the nasal vowels /ɛ̃ œ̃ ɑ̃ ɔ̃/ are (intrinsically) long in closed syllables and therefore not subject to laxing either. Consequently, the intrinsically long vowels, vowels followed by /v z ʒ r/ and any vowel participating in an opposition of tense versus lax will not undergo vowel laxing in CF. Part (b) of (10) summarizes this situation.

(10) CF VOWEL PHONEMES

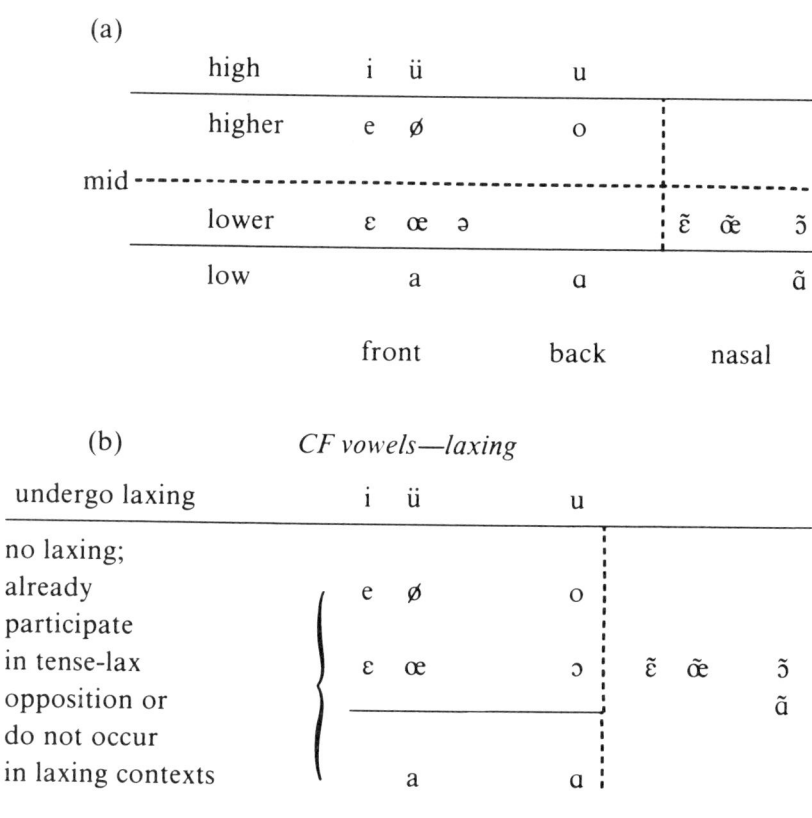

(a)

		front			back		nasal		
	high	i	ü		u				
	higher	e	ø		o				
mid									
	lower	ɛ	œ	ə			ɛ̃	œ̃	ɔ̃
	low	a			ɑ		ɑ̃		

(b)   *CF vowels—laxing*

undergo laxing	i	ü		u				
no laxing; already participate in tense-lax opposition or do not occur in laxing contexts	e ɛ	ø œ		o ɔ		ɛ̃	œ̃	ɔ̃ ɑ̃
	a			ɑ				

no laxing; intrinsically long

In the context of (10b), the laxing rule for stressed vowels may be limited to high vowels. It is given in (11).

(11) *Vowel laxing—stressed vowels*

$$\begin{bmatrix} V \\ +high \\ -mid \\ +stress \end{bmatrix} \rightarrow [-tense] / \_\_ C_x \#$$

(where "x" refers to all CF consonants except /v z ʒ r/ i.e. to non-lengthening consonants)

Stressed high vowels are lax in final syllables, if the syllable is not closed by a lengthening consonant.

In fact, we have not yet exhausted the problems associated with vowel laxing, because of the behaviour of forms like those in (12), where the vowel in the left-hand column is also lax:

(12)
infirme	[ɛ̃fIrm]			
absurde	[apsÜrd]			
purge	[pÜrʒ]			
hurle	[Ürl]			
sourde	[sUrd]	versus	sourd	[suːr]
lourde	[lUrd]		lourd	[luːr]
courte	[kUrt]		court	[kuːr]
course	[kUrs]		cours	[kuːr]

Thus, if the C_x of rule (9) is followed by another consonant, laxing may still take place. This difficulty can be avoided if we take advantage of the interaction between lengthening and laxing by invoking the principle of rule ordering between the lengthening processes (7a-b above) and laxing (11). If lengthening applies first, then laxing may be constrained to affect only *short* high vowels, all others having been removed from its domain by previous lengthening. Provided that lengthening has first applied, laxing may then be stated as in (13):

(13) *Vowel Laxing*

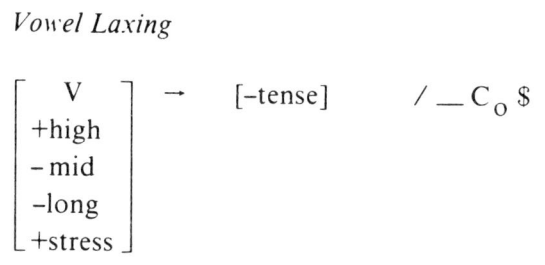

$$\begin{bmatrix} V \\ +\text{high} \\ -\text{mid} \\ -\text{long} \\ +\text{stress} \end{bmatrix} \rightarrow [-\text{tense}] \quad / \_\_ C_0 \$$$

Short high vowels are lax in final closed syllables (and there are no longer any restrictions on the type of syllable-final consonant).

(14) | *Examples*: | *vire* | *ville* | *courbe* |
      |---|---|---|---|
      | lengthening | i: | — | — |
      | laxing | — | I | U |

3.2.1 *Pretonic laxing*

The laxing rule we have discussed up to this point involves stressed vowels, and is obligatory. There is a closely related process, however, that laxes high vowels in pretonic closed syllables, this time in a variable but frequent fashion. Consider such forms as those in (15):

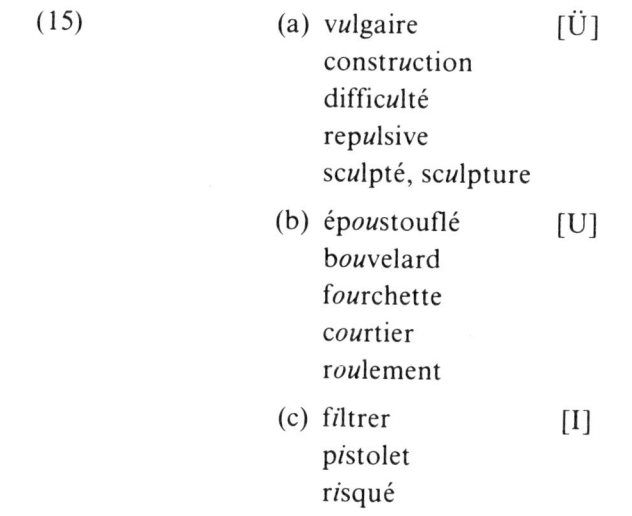

(15) (a) v*u*lgaire   [Ü]
          constr*u*ction
          diffic*u*lté
          rep*u*lsive
          sc*u*lpté, sc*u*lpture

      (b) ép*ou*stouflé   [U]
          b*ou*velard
          f*ou*rchette
          c*ou*rtier
          r*ou*lement

      (c) f*i*ltrer   [I]
          p*i*stolet
          r*i*squé

where again there may be variation in the degree to which certain words are susceptible to pretonic laxing. (A *consonne allongeante*, for example, seems to hinder, without completely blocking, this laxing: *purement, amusement, jugement.*) We may formulate this rule as in (16a); the similarity to (13) is evident. In fact, the two laxing rules may even be combined into the single format (16b), if we add the condition that (16b) is obligatory in final syllables, and optional in non-final contexts. One would then be able to see (16b) as a generalization of (13) and (16a) through a relaxation of the conditions that limit the applicability of the two former rules, i.e. through an extension of the contexts in which they apply. Both rules, Pretonic Laxing and the generalized High Vowel Laxing, follow.

(16)   (a) *Pretonic Laxing (optional)*

$$\begin{bmatrix} V \\ +high \\ -mid \\ -long \\ -stress \end{bmatrix} \rightarrow [-tense] \quad / \_\_ C_o \$$$

Short high vowels may be lax in pretonic closed syllables.

(b) *High Vowel Laxing (generalized)*

$$\begin{bmatrix} V \\ +high \\ -mid \\ -long \end{bmatrix} \rightarrow [-tense] \quad / \_\_ C_o \$$$

Short high vowels lax in closed syllables (optional for unstressed vowels; obligatory for stressed vowels).

From the preceding discussion, we have excluded a set of exceptions to laxing—exceptions supplied by English loanwords containing high vowels in closed syllables, as in (17).

(17)

	mean	[min]
	cheap	[čip]
	(blue) jeans	[ǰin]
	suit	[sut]
	boost	[bus]
	boom	[bum]

In certain cases, these loans may introduce a phonemic distinction linked to the difference between native and loan vocabulary.

(18)

	mean	[min]	mine	[mIn]
	jeans	[ǰin]	fine	[fIn]
	suit	[sut]	route	[rUt]
	boost	[bus]	pousse	[pUs]
	boom	[bum]	boum	[bUm]

However, the fact that certain of these English loans fluctuate in CF between a tense and a lax V, in spite of a tense vowel in the English source word, and the fact that others have been completely naturalized to contain a lax V (Gendron 1967), indicate the direction of evolution, the structure of the CF system and one possible outcome for all of the loans.

(19)   (a) *reel*   [ril – rIl]
                     speech   [spič – spIč]
                       seal   [sil – sIl]

(b) *team*   [t^{S}Im]
   steam   [st^{S}Im]
   bean   [bIn]
   beam   [bIm]
   loose   [lUs]
   caboose [kabUs]
   baloon [balUn]

Given current changes in the behaviour of long vowels (particularly pretonic vowels), as well as the existence of certain lax vowels before lengthening consonants in loan words (*quiz* [kwIz]), it is perhaps premature, in the absence of systematic bodies of data, to speculate further on the status of the tense-lax distinction in CF.

Finally, we may note an interesting phenomenon involving the role of word boundaries in conditioning laxing. In pairs such as *petit ami* versus *petite amie*, pronounced as [pt^{S}itami] versus [pt^{S}Itami], we see that in spite of the same syllabification, the feminine form contains a lax vowel [I] while the masculine form contains tense [i]. There are several theoretical difficulties with such pairs, difficulties which go beyond the bounds of this discussion. Suffice it to note that the key to the problem involves the liaison consonant *t* in *petit*, and that we have here another example of the special status of such consonants in French phonology. This type of example can be extended to cover lengthening as well as laxing. Recall that in *court*, the /u/ is long, while it is short and consequently lax in *courte*. But in sequences like *à court terme*, the vowel remains long, despite the presence of /t/, because of the intervening word boundary. We then have contrasts such as those in (20),

(20)   *un court appel*   [kuːrapɛl]
       une courte absence   [kUrtapsɑ̃s]
       à court terme   [akuːrtɛrm]

where the tense and lax (long and short) vowels contrast in identical segmental contexts, but where the morphological structure and position of the /t/ relative to the word boundary play a crucial role. We will return later to a brief consideration of the role of the word in CF phonology.

3.2.2 *Laxing harmony*

Closed syllables do not provide the only context in which lax vowels occur in CF. There is a second process, called laxing harmony, by means of which pretonic high vowels in open syllables may optionally become lax. The process appears to be favoured in initial syllables or if the following syllable contains a lax vowel. Consider the forms in (21).

(21)
	abusif	[abÜzIf]
	bicycle	[bIsIk]
	choucroute	[ʃUkrUt]
	clinique	[klInIk]
	communisme	[kɔmÜnIs]
	cousine	[kUzIn]
	coutume	[kUt^{S}Üm]
	définitif	[defInIt^{S}If]
	difficile	[d^{Z}IfIsIl]
	habitude	[abIt^{S}Üd]
	inutile	[InÜt^{S}Il]
	juridique	[ʒÜrId^{Z}Ik]
	ministre	[mInIs]
	ministère	[mInIstɛːr – mInistɛːr]
	minute	[mInÜt]
	Philippe	[fIlIp]
	pilule	[pIlÜl]
	pupitre	[pÜpIt]
	scrupule	[skrÜpÜl]
	soucoupe	[sUkUp]
	touriste	[tUrIs]
	unique	[ÜnIk]

In each form in (21), the vowel in the final syllable will have been obligatorily laxed by the laxing rule (13), and these lax vowels no doubt have a harmonizing or assimilatory influence on the vowels preceding them. We will, however, need a further rule to lax the pretonic vowels of (21). What are the conditions on this rule? Note first that, because both [fiIp] and [fIIp] are acceptable pronunciations for *Philippe* in the dialect in question (although the latter is much more frequent), the rule must be variable. That is, in order to account for the variation between tense and lax pretonic vowels, the rule may apply in some cases (when the vowel is to appear as lax) and fail to apply in others. As is typical with variable rules, there may be a considerable amount of individual, social or regional variation in their application. It is clear, furthermore, that certain words are resistant to laxing (words with a "learned" flavour, such as *primitif*, *unique*, *typique*, *humide*), while in others (i.e. *pupitre*) harmony applies in almost categorical fashion. We will see further examples of this differential application of variable rules in sections to follow.

Secondly, the fact that the rule is one of harmony, often depending on the presence of a lax vowel in following syllables, can be seen in the data of (22), where the rule may fail to apply if a following lax vowel is absent. (If the vowel of the initial syllable does lax, we will attribute this to a separate optional rule laxing high vowels in initial open syllables.)

(22)

musique	[mÜzIk]	*musicien*	[müzisjẽ – mÜzisjẽ]
cuisine	[kqIzIn]	*cuisiner*	[kqizine – kqIzine]
ministre	[mInIs]	*ministère*	[ministɛ:r – mInistɛ:r]
scrupule	[skrÜpÜl]	*scrupuleux*	[skrüpülø – skrÜpÜlø]
positif	[pɔzIt^{S}If]	*positive*	[pɔzit^{S}i:v]
primitif	[prImIt^{S}if]	*primitive*	[primit^{S}i:v – prImit^{S}i:v]
		difficile	[d^{Z}ifisIl – d^{Z}IfisIl]

These remarks permit us to formalize Laxing Harmony in the following way, incorporating the conditions we have sketched in the preceding paragraphs:

(23) (a) *Laxing Harmony (optional)*

$$\begin{bmatrix} V \\ +high \end{bmatrix} \rightarrow [-tense] \quad / \_\_ \$ C_0 \begin{bmatrix} V \\ -tense \end{bmatrix}$$

High vowels may lax in open syllables when the following syllable contains a lax vowel.

(b) *Initial Syllable Laxing (optional)*

$$\begin{bmatrix} V \\ +high \end{bmatrix} \rightarrow [-tense] \quad / \# C_0 \_\_ \$$$

High vowels may lax in initial open syllables.

In a formalized grammar, Laxing Harmony (23a) would be required to follow Laxing (16), since the latter process creates the lax vowels which condition harmonization. The order of Laxing Harmony with respect to Pretonic Laxing is irrelevant, since the rules are formulated in such a way as to affect different types of syllables, Laxing Harmony and Initial Syllable Laxing applying in open syllables and Pretonic Laxing in closed. There are, however, cases where the laxing rules overlap, depending on the placement of the syllable boundary. However, since the vowel would lax by either rule, this does not constitute a problem for the analysis presented here, although the whole question of vowel laxing in CF remains one where much further work is needed.

We are now in a position to summarize the processes of vowel laxing in CF: Laxing, Pretonic Laxing, Laxing Harmony, and Initial Syllable Laxing. The first two affect high vowels in closed syllables, stressed and unstressed respectively. The third and fourth operate in pretonic open syllables. The last three rules are optional or variable, with all the social, individual, lexical or geographic fluctuation implied by the term. Laxing, however, is obligatory in the dialect in question, although it may be consciously over-ridden if the speaker attempts to switch to a more formal register. The examples of (24) indicate the application of the rules.

(24)   (a) *Laxing*   (b) *Pretonic Laxing*
       vite   vulgaire
       flute   boulevard
       musique   pistolet

    (c) *Laxing Harmony*   (d) *Initial Syllable Laxing*
       positif   musique
       difficile   numéro
       primitif   bubonique
       habitude   cuisinier

    In words of only two syllables where the second syllable contains a lax vowel, either Laxing Harmony or Initial Syllable Laxing could account for the quality of the vowel in the initial syllable: musique, cuisine, etc.

Each of the processes in (22) affects short vowels,[3] most often in what may be considered a weak position (closed or unstressed syllable). Let us now examine certain phenomena that systematically affect long vowels.

3.3   *Diphthongization*

If by "weakening" one understands laxing, devoicing or deletion, then short vowels are frequently weakened in CF. Long vowels, on the other hand, undergo a converse type of modification, strengthening through diphthongization. ("Strengthening" is not necessarily to be interpreted literally here, although it is clear

---

   3. Note that if a short vowel in a position to become lax is exceptionally lengthened in pretonic position (in expressive speech, for example) laxing becomes impossible: *stupide* [stˢüpId]: *que t'es stupide!* [... stˢü:pId], never *[stˢÜ̱:pId].

that diphthongization renders vowels perceptually more distinct.) Diphthongization in this case consists of adding to the vowel a following semi-vowel that agrees with that vowel in frontness and rounding. The off-glides involved, therefore, are the three CF semi-vowels /j ɥ w/. Consider the examples of diphthongs in stressed position in (25).

(25) *Diphthongal realizations of CF vowels*

/i/	[ij]	/ü/	[üɥ]	/u/	[uw]
	vire		pur		tour
	arrive		juge		rouge
/e/	[ej]	/ø/	[øɥ]	/o/	[ow]
	neige		neutre		chaude
	steak		jeûne		côte
/ɛ/	[ɛj] / [aj]	/œ/	[œɥ]	/ɔ/	[ɔw]
	père		beurre		port
	neige		peur		fort
/a/		/ɑ/	[ɑw]		
			pâte		
			part		
/ɛ̃/	[ɛ̃j]	/œ̃/	[œ̃ɥ]	/ɔ̃/	[ɔ̃w]
	crainte		défunte		honte
	teinte		emprunte		ombre
		/ɑ̃/	[ɑ̃w]		
			lente		
			trempe		

As the examples indicate, a vowel may have a diphthongal variant either if it is lengthened by a *consonne allongeante* (*tour, fort*) or if it is intrinsically long (*chaude, honte*). The different causes of length have no effect on the type of diphthongization produced, even if the vowel in question happens to be long both intrinsically and by position (i.e. *chose*).

This table calls for several comments. Note first that, compared to the inventory of vowel phonemes in (3) of Chapter 2, there are several gaps in the set of vowels undergoing diphthongization. For each of these, however, there is a clear explanation in terms of the structure of CF phonology. The neutral vowel /ə/, for example, is not included since it rarely occurs in closed syllables,[4] consequently cannot be long, and is never stressed. Nor does /a/ diphthongize, although on occasion it may merge with /ɑ/, which does diphthongize. The reasons for this exceptional status of /a/ with respect to diphthongization remain obscure. Finally, /e/ is excluded from closed syllables in SF, and largely from the same context in CF, particularly in native words. There is, however, a limited set of words in CF, occasionally indigenous but particularly including English loans, containing /e/ in a closed syllable, and here the vowel follows the appropriate diphthongizing pattern: *neige* [nejʒ], *mère* [mejr], *brake* [brejk], *date* [dejt], *steak* [stejk] and so on. Aside from these three exclusions, all CF vowels may diphthongize given the appropriate circumstances. Note that we are dealing with the structure of the CF vowel system, not with the number of examples. Thus, the number of words in *eC$*, i.e. with /e/ in a closed syllable, is small (and is limited largely to loan words), but those words which do occur are perfectly regular in their behaviour, diphthongizing to [ej]. Exactly the same holds for (native) words in *œC$*, which are also exceedingly rare. The examples given (*défunte*, *emprunte*) are perhaps the only two extant, yet they follow the same regular pattern as all the other vowels, and are in no way exceptional.

The preceding discussion involves systematic gaps in diphthongization, as it were. There are also more specific exclusions among the diphthongs, this time involving the following segmental context rather that the diphthong itself. The vowel /ɔ/, for example, never diphthongizes before /z/ for the simple reason that, due to the phonotactic constraints of French, it never occurs there. On the other hand /ɔ/ does occur before /ʒ/ (*horloge*, *éloge*, *toge* etc.), but here too diphthongization is blocked. We never find, that

---

4. A few exceptions to this generalization will have to be recognized in metathesized forms such as *bertelles* for *bretelles*, or *le* in clitic constructions such as *envie de le faire* /ãvidəlfajr/ (see section 3.10). In neither case, however, does diphthongization ever occcur.

is, [ɔw] before /ʒ/. In the same vein, /ɛ/ is fairly frequent before /v/, but except for a very small set of exceptions,[5] no diphthongization occurs. We do not find, for example, *[grajv] for *grève*, only [grɛːv]. Finally, diphthongization is variable for the vowel /ɑ/ before /v/ and /ʒ/. There are certain words, such as *cadavre*, *âge*, where a diphthong seems obligatory, but the vast majority of words appear to allow [aː] or [ɑw] interchangeably. We will not speculate concerning the source of the exceptions of note 5, nor of the variability involved, except to remark that both seem typical of the progress of variable rules and of lexical diffusion. Dumas (1974b) offers some discussion of this matter.

To summarize, then, consider the chart in (26) of diphthongized variants of long vowels compared to the "normal" vowel (see also (25)).

(26)   DIPHTHONGS IN CF

i – Ij	ü – Üɥ	u – Uw
e – ej	ø – øɥ	o – ow
ɛ – ɛj/aj	œ – œɥ	ɔ – ɔw
	ɑ – ɑw	
ɛ̃ – ɛ̃j	œ̃ – œ̃ɥ	ɔ̃ – ɔ̃w
	ɑ̃ – ɑ̃w	

The chart in (26) brings out the relationship between the diphthongized and the non-diphthongized variants of all vowels. There still remain, however, several points of phonetic detail to be

---

5. They are five in number (cf. Dumas 1974b): *fève*, *rêve*, *orfèvre*, *poivre* and *Lefebvre*, all with [aj]. Santerre 1976d attributes this behaviour to a long underlying vowel (/ɛː/) in these forms, while the vowel that does not diphthongize is /ɛ/, which has been lengthened by the /v/, one of the *consonnes allongeantes*.

clarified. First among these is the precise phonetic nature of the diphthongs. Let us first consider the high vowels /i ü u/. Here the nucleus of the diphthong is indicated in detail as a lowered, laxer variant of the non-diphthongized counterpart [i-I, ü-Ü, u-U], while the off-glide is a standard semi-vowel. This type of differentiation is fairly common within complex vowel nuclei, since the greater the articulatory (and perceptual) difference between the nucleus and the off-glide, the greater will be the impression of the diphthongal quality of the segment as a whole. The movement from [I] to [j], for example, is more distinct than that from [i] to [j], and the lowered nuclei in CF diphthongs serve to emphasize their changing quality.[6]

The higher-mid and nasalized vowels present perhaps the clearest match between the simple and diphthongized vowels, and require no further comment other than to say that, in a fashion similar to /i ü u/, the vowels /e ø o/ may reinforce their diphthongal quality (in phonetic terms) by also having lowered nuclei combined with the off-glides: [e-ɛj, ø-œɥ, o-ɔw]. The lower-mid vowels, on the other hand, present several complexities, the most evident of which is the great variation in the diphthongal realizations of /ɛ/. What we have noted as [ɛj] or [aj] may, in fact, appear as [aj], [ɛj] or [ej] (with various intermediate versions), depending on a variety of factors including region, social class, age or sex. There may also be phonological conditioning, such as degree of stress, at work. Nor is it excluded that certain lexical items present one variant, while others are characterized by a different nucleus. Once again, such fluctuation is inherent in the nature of variable rules. It is particularly active in the structure of the CF linguistic system, which is undergoing a set of pressures, both internal and external, to change.

Nor is it just the front vowel /ɛ/ which presents this phonetic variation. The back vowels also do so, and corresponding to /ɑ/ and /ɔ/ we may find variants ranging from [ɑw] through [ɑᵒ] to [aw] and [aᵒ] for the former and [ɑᵒ, ɑᵓ, ɔᵒ] or [aᵒ] for the

---

6. Consider, in this context, the difference between the English diphthongs /ij – ej/ or /uw – ow/ (*beat-bait, boot-boat,* etc.), where it is often difficult to convince English speakers of the diphthongal nature of the first member of each pair.

latter (see Santerre 1974, among others). These examples illustrate a phenomenon affecting the off-glides of certain CF diphthongs, namely the fact that such off-glides need not be fully closed semi-vowels, but may instead be non-syllabic but lower glides. In fact, the same applies to the realizations of diphthongized /ɛ/ where one of the most frequent alternates is [a^{ɛ}]. Note that the lower off-glides are present only with the lower vowel nuclei; again we see how the mutual relations between the elements of a diphthong may influence the phonetic realizations of the two (or more) parts of complex syllabic nuclei. Be that as it may, for convenience we will continue to represent the CF diphthongs using standard semi-vowel symbols, but the use of such notation to englobe a wide variety of phonetic diversity should be recalled. Against this background, and ignoring the finer phonetic detail, we may work with the following diphthongization rule:

(27) DIPHTHONGIZATION IN CF

$$\emptyset \rightarrow \begin{bmatrix} G \\ \alpha \text{ back} \\ \beta \text{ round} \end{bmatrix} / \begin{bmatrix} V \\ + \text{stress} \\ + \text{long} \\ \alpha \text{ back} \\ \beta \text{ round} \end{bmatrix} \underline{\quad}$$

A glide agreeing with the nucleus in backness and rounding is inserted following long stressed vowels.

So far, we have considered diphthongs only in tonic (stressed) position. This is fully understandable given the relation between length and diphthongization: only long vowels diphthongize and long vowels are normally found under stress. But we have already seen that, in certain circumstances at least, long vowels may occur in pretonic position in CF, albeit in a variable fashion. As a consequence, it is possible to find pretonic diphthongs in CF, although such diphthongs must be considered a relatively infrequent variant of long vowels in that position. Consider the examples of (28):

(28) *il est bien fâché*   [... fɑwʃe]
      je comprends   [kɔ̃wprɑ̃]
      calice   [kɑwlIs]   (both
        or   [kɑwlIn]   exclamations)
      il est tout mêlé   [... mejle]
      il est barré   [... bɑwre]
      sablé   [sɑwble]

However, given the frequency of stress retraction and of the "accent d'insistance" in popular spoken French, one may also consider that such forms as those in (28) are accented on the initial syllable, and that consequently the link between stress, length and diphthongization is preserved. In any case, these forms are a function of the variability of all three processes of pretonic length, stress shift and diphthongization in non-final syllables, so their lesser frequency is fully comprehensible.[7]

We may now consider, on a more abstract level, the link between diphthongization on the one hand and laxing on the other. In the distribution of energy over longer phonological sequences, it is often the case that there is an alternation between strong and weak syllables. Consider, for example, the pattern of alternating stress and reduced vowels in such English words as *photographic* [fòtəgræfIk], *communication* [kəmjùnəkéjʃən] and so on. Such patterning is no doubt linked to general rhythmic and perceptual principles underlying much articulatory activity. In any case, in languages with final stress, word-final syllables and, to a lesser extent, word-initial syllables are considered to be strong positions, while word-internal contexts are weak. In the same vein, long vowels are stronger than short ones. Furthermore, there may be a tendency over time (or in synchronic variation) to reinforce stronger syllables and to further weaken those of lesser prominence, particularly where there is an alternating strong-weak (or

---

7. Note also the particular intonation contour that normally accompanies these "pretonic" diphthongs; a rising-falling pattern distributed over the syllable: [kɑ̂wlIs], [kɔ̃̂wprɑ̃], etc.

weak-strong) pattern. (For further discussion of a theory of historical phonology based on such principles, see Foley 1977).

Against this background, how may we interpret the CF phenomena we have been discussing? To begin with, it is clear that diphthongization represents a further strengthening of already strong segments. The fact that diphthongization affects long vowels, under stress in the vast majority of cases, is sufficient to demonstrate this, particularly since the perceptual prominence of these vowels is also heightened by their diphthongal quality. Conversely, laxing is strongly linked to short vowels, and may be seen as a further gesture toward emphasizing the difference between strong and weak syllables. We must note, however, that laxing occurs in both stressed and unstressed syllables, so the exclusive link between strong and weak is lessened in this case. Nevertheless, the fact remains that it is the high vowels which lax in CF. In terms of the strength hierarchies developed by Foley (1977:44–48), the high vowels are the weakest among the vowels, so we have a further example of a weakening process preferentially affecting the weakest elements in the system.

This example serves to illustrate the complexity of the problem of natural tendencies (or of linguistic universals in general), since to every claim there may exist several countervailing or complementary processes. Here, for example, we may be dealing with more than one type of laxing, linked to syllable structure on the one hand (lax vowels are often associated with closed syllables) and to general assimilatory principles (vowel harmony is a type of assimilation). When questions of stress, rhythm, syllable structure and assimilation are involved, there is clearly more than one possible outcome. But it remains evident that diphthongization is clearly a type of strengthening in the CF context, in that it hypercharacterizes length, and that laxing, or at least part of the laxing process, is complementary to diphthongization in that it highlights shortness and heightens the strong-weak contrast between syllables. (Dumas 1978 presents an alternative but not unrelated analysis of the links between diphthongization and laxing in terms of the notion of phonological tension.) We will see further manifestations of phonological weakening in the material to follow.

3.4 Devoicing

Voiceless vowels are rare in the languages of the world, and it is doubtful that there exists anywhere a full-blown phonemic distinction between voiced and voiceless vowels. Given the extreme difficulty in perceiving and distinguishing such segments, this is not surprising. Voiceless allophones, however, may arise in various contexts, again as a result of general assimilatory or weakening processes. Such is the case for the voiceless vowels in CF. We will not consider here the general assimilation of voicing in glides (and other sonorants) preceded by voiceless obstruents: p*i*ed, t*u*er, c*oi*n and so on. This process is common to all French dialects, and does not serve to distinguish CF from other varieties. Consider the examples in (29).

(29) équ*i*per, -age /i/
étiquette
inc*i*ter
conf*i*ture
class*i*fier
just*i*fication
équ*i*té
prat*i*quer
prof*i*table
dép*u*té /ü/
disp*u*té
occ*u*pé, occ*u*pation, préocc*u*pé
cap*u*cin
amp*u*té
déc*ou*per, -age /u/
éc*ou*ter

In each of these examples, the italicized vowel, that of the second syllable, is realized without vibration of the vocal cords. (In terms of the length of the words, measured either instrumentally or by asking native speakers how many syllables they contain, there is clearly a vowel present.) The conditions governing this devoicing process, therefore, appear to be the following: (a) Devoicing affects the high vowels /i ü u/ only (vowels in such words as *incapable*, *détester* do not devoice). (b) The vowel must be in weak position, i.e. in an inter-tonic or word medial syllable. Vowels in initial or final syllables are not usually affected. (c) The surrounding context preferably consists of voiceless obstruents; a preceding or following voiced segment is sufficient to interfere with the process. (d) In cases where there are two inter-tonic vowels meeting the conditions for devoicing (as in class*i*fication, inst*i*tution, const*i*tution, for example) both vowels may be devoiced. Given this set of constraints, we may formalize the rule as in (30).

(30) VOWEL DEVOICING

$$\begin{bmatrix} V \\ +high \end{bmatrix} \rightarrow [-voice] \; / C_0 \, V \, C_0 \begin{bmatrix} -son \\ -voice \end{bmatrix} - \begin{bmatrix} -son \\ -voice \end{bmatrix} C_0 \, V \, C_0$$

High vowels devoice in word medial syllables when surrounded by voiceless consonants.[8]

Given the perceptual difficulties engendered by such a process, it is clear we are dealing with another weakening phenomenon. The fact that high vowels are again the input to the rule and that the rule affects vowels in weak position confirms this analysis. We must point out, however, that the situation is not quite as clear-cut as (30) implies. While this formulation represents the main attributes of devoicing in CF, there are a few situations where we must note exceptions or irregular behaviour. From the little published data available on this process, i.e. Gendron 1966a: 45–55, Charbonneau 1955, it is evident that here again we are investigating a variable phenomenon. We have already seen the "frayed edges" of other such processes, and the same type of behaviour should not surprise us in this domain. In each case, the

---

8. In formal terms, this rule must apply to both medial vowels in a # $C_0 V C_0 V C_0 V C_0$ # sequence, if the conditions (a) and (c) are met. For the formal mechanisms assuring this type of application, see Chomsky and Halle 1968.

irregularities involve extension of the devoicing process beyond the constraints imposed by (30). There are, for example, cases of devoicing in initial syllables: c*ou*pale, p*u*pitre, p*i*toune, s*i* tu veux, etc. We also find examples of devoicing where one of the consonants in the environment is voiced: synd*i*cat, éd*i*fice. But only very rarely do we find exceptions where more than one of the conditions is violated; *bistro* [bi̥stro] devoices in an initial syllable with an initial voiced consonant, but forms like *ambigu* do not show devoicing.

Finally, we may note that word boundaries, here as elsewhere, interfere with the devoicing process. The devoicing in (31) is less frequent than that in the word-internal contexts of (30).

(31)   (a) une sort*ie* # privée
un tax*i* # tout sale
beauc*ou*p # trop
surt*ou*t # pas
c'est romp*u* # tout ça
il est têt*u* # ton ami

(b) cette # h*i*stoire
chaque # h*i*ppy
sept # *ou*tils
presque # *ou*tré
ils sont tous # *u*tilisés
chaque # *u*stensile

In (31a), one could claim that the presence of a residual word stress, even within the larger phrase, also inhibits devoicing. The (b) forms, on the other hand, present no such possibility, and we must again recognize the crucial role of word boundaries in CF phonology, since the boundary again blocks a phonological process. (Note that we have excluded examples like *ces # piquets*, where the voiceless consonant follows the word boundary. In such cases, any devoicing could be attributed to the exceptional extension of devoicing to initial syllables discussed above.)

3.5 Vowel deletion

Laxing and devoicing are different manifestations of weakening in vowels. The ultimate stage, however, can only be complete disappearance of the segments involved. Such deletion also occurs in CF as the examples of (32) testify (cf. Santerre 1975, Gendron 1966a: 150-151).

(32)   (a) *proføsseur*
électricı̸té
universı̸té
de la chı̸cane
le vı̸sage
musı̸cal

    (b) *comı̸té*
polı̸tique
les rı̸chesses
pas nøcessaire
habilı̸té
c'est cømmode
orøı̸ller
magnı̸fique

    (c) *pı̸scine*
bı̸zarre
quı̸ c'est
popи̸lation
tapı̸sser
déguı̸ser

It is possible, from these examples, to find three principal types of context in which vowel deletion takes place. In (a), deletion occurs when there is a preceding fricative; in (b), a sonorant (nasal or liquid) precedes; while in (c), the vowel deletes between a stop and a fricative. Other factors also seem to play a role: deletion affects inter-tonic vowels, weak by position, in (a), (b), and sometimes in (c). In addition, where there is no fricative or sonorant available to "absorb" the vowel, as in (c), we find that deletion favours very strongly the high vowel /i/ (as well as (/ü, u/)), which we have already seen to undergo other weakening processes.

It is also the case that deletion is highly variable, even within the same speaker, depending on style and context. Such rules are often difficult to formalize, particularly if one attempts to incorporate every detail which may be relevant. Nevertheless, an initial attempt is found in (33), based on the material in Santerre 1975, by far the most complete and detailed discussion of the question to date (see also Santerre and Dufour 1983, Cedergren 1983).

(33) VOWEL DELETION (VARIABLE)

$$V \rightarrow \emptyset\ /\ \#\ C_0\ \underset{1}{(VC)}\ \_\$\ \underset{2}{C\ V}$$

Conditions: Deletion is favoured when the vowel is high, when 1 is a sonorant consonant, when 2 is a fricative, and when the word is long.

Vowels delete optionally in medial syllables in sonorant contexts.

Finally, we should note that deletion of a vowel may provoke additional changes in certain forms, specifically the compensatory lengthening of preceding fricatives, as indicated in the examples in (34).

(34)
	électricité	[elɛktris:te]
	université	[ünivɛrs:te]
	citation	[s:tɑ:sjɔ̃]
	il est supposé	[jes:po:ze]
	préciser	[pres:ze]

We will attempt no formulation of this rule here. Although it is formally straightforward, the conditions that would have to be placed on its application would lead us too far afield.[9] Instead, we may leave the general domain of weakening and strengthening of vowel realizations, and turn to the behaviour of the low vowels in CF.

3.6   *The low vowels /a/ and /ɑ/*

We have already seen an active opposition in CF between /ɛ/ and /ɛ:/, contrary to SF where any phonemic opposition of length is exceedingly rare. Much the same situation obtains in the case of /a/ versus /ɑ/ in CF. Unlike SF, where again there is a tendency for many occurrences of these vowels to fluctuate or for merger to take place (at least in middle and upper class speech, see Mettas 1970, Lennig 1978), the CF opposition is very much alive, and is reinforced by certain additional modifications that have occurred. This does not mean that the CF situation is without its own complications, which we will attempt to treat systematically in what follows. The best starting point is in the closed-syllable, non-lengthening context, illustrated in (35).

(35)   /a/   /ɑ/

      cap   râpe   Context: / __ C_o #
      lac   Jacques   (where C_o is non-
      lame   âme   lengthening)
      canne   âne
      tache   tâche
      malle   mâle

In this case, the /a/ is usually realized as a fronted allophone [æ] as in *patte* [pæt]. The vowel /ɑ/, on the other hand,

---

9. Specifically, we would have to decide whether the effects of this rule should be incorporated into vowel deletion as a type of compensatory lengthening, or whether it should remain an independent rule constrained to apply only in derived contexts, but not in forms like *station* *[sstɑsjɔ̃], where no vowel deletion has occurred.

is one of the intrinsically long vowels, and in the closed syllables of (33) would normally be long and diphthongized: [pɑwt, ʒɑwk, ɑwm] for *pâte, Jacques, âme* and so on. Thus the /a/ – /ɑ/ distinction is reinforced in phonetic terms by the fronting of /a/ and the lengthening and diphthongization of /ɑ/ (see in this connection Bossé and Dugas 1983).

Let us now turn to the behaviour of the vowels in final open syllables, where any length differences would be neutralized. (Long vowels occur only in *closed* final syllables in French.) Consider the examples in (36).

(36) (a) /ɑ/ Context: / __ #   (b) /a/ – /ɑ/

       gras – grasse   *chatte – chat*
       bas – basse   *tabagie – tabac*
       voix – voisé   *plate – plat*
       tas – entasser   *draperie – drap*
       repas   *abattoir – abat*
       ananas   *éclater – éclat*
       cadenas   *garçon – gars*
                               débattre – débat
                               ingrate – ingrat
                               sénateur – sénat

Consider first the words in (36a). Here, the basic vowel of the stem is /ɑ/, whether it occurs in absolute word-final position (*gras*), in a final closed syllable (*grasse*) or word-internally (*entasser*). The vowel, in other words, is unchanging in all contexts. The items in (36b), however, are different. Here, we see related words (masculine – feminine, verb – noun, noun – derived noun) where the vowel /ɑ/ occurs in final open syllables (*chat*, etc.), but where the front vowel /a/ occurs elsewhere (*chatte* /ʃat/, *éclater* /eklate/ and so on). The reason for the vowel change in (36b) is that CF does not permit the occurrence of /a/ in final open syllables. (We will discuss later certain conditions on this statement, which should be taken to exclude the diphthong *oi*, /wa/ ~ /wɑ/.) Consequently, the underlying vowel /a/ of the forms in (36b) must be modified to /ɑ/ in final open syllables. This is accomplished through a process of vowel backing, described in (37), which reflects partially the constraints on /a/ in CF.

(37) BACKING (MINOR)

$$\begin{bmatrix} V \\ +\text{low} \\ +\text{stress} \end{bmatrix} \rightarrow [+\text{back}] \ / \_\_ \#$$

All low vowels are back in final open syllables.

In structural terms, we are dealing with the partial neutralization of the /a/ – /ɑ/ opposition in final open syllables, and (37) is a neutralization rule. As illustrated above, this neutralization introduces a morphophonemic alternation into stems such as those of (36b). Finally, we should note that in phonetic terms, there are further modifications to consider. The realization of the neutralized opposition may vary from [ɑ] to [ɒ] to [ɔ]. This further shift entails no additional merger with /ɔ/, however, since the phoneme /ɔ/ is excluded from final position in both SF and CF. Any phonetic segment [ɔ] in that position, therefore, must be an allophone of /ɑ/.

We said earlier that the backing rule involved only partial neutralization. On the one hand, a small set of reduplicative forms, illustrated in (38), shows the vowel /a/ word-finally. Given the idiosyncratic phonological and semantic nature of these forms, there is nothing surprising in this behaviour.

(38)   *papa*   /papa/   */papɑ/ etc.
            dada   /dada/
            caca   /kaka/
            nana   /nana/

The second set of contrastive items is more interesting, since it shows the crucial role of stress in the backing rule. In (39), we find the same morpheme in two contexts, one stressed, one unstressed, or we find proclitics which can never receive stress. In neither case does backing affect the unstressed form.

(39) (a) *ça fait mal*   /sa̱fɛmal/
      ça, j'aime ça   /saʒɛmsɑ/
      (b) *ma maison*   /ma̱mezɔ̃/
      la table   /la̱tab/
      jusqu'à date   /ʒüska̱dat/

Let us now turn to perhaps the most complicated type of behaviour involving the low vowels—that found in lengthening contexts, i.e. preceding the consonants /v z ʒ r/. In SF, as represented by Juilland (1965) or Walter (1976), there are few examples of any opposition between /a/ and /ɑ/ in lengthening contexts. The reason for this absence, moreover, is not hard to discern. If, in phonetic terms, /ɑ/ is usually distinguished from /a/ by both quality and length, the fact that both are long in the contexts in question (/a/ by the *consonne allongeante*, /ɑ/ because of its intrinsic length) reduces the possibilities for any viable distinction. Reflecting this, in Juilland (1965) there are no occurrences of /ɑ/ before /ʒ/, and virtually none before /v/ and /r/. Excluding *oi* (/wa/), to which we will devote a separate section, there are very few /a/ to be found preceding /z/, where /ɑ/ predominates. (As exceptions, we may cite the forms *hâve*, *croire*, *accroire* and *cadavre* with /ɑ/; *topaze* with /a/.) Walter lists more "exceptions" to these statements than does Juilland, but the generalizations appear relatively firm. The words in (40) are representative of the SF distribution of /a/ and /ɑ/ in lengthening contexts, where we find /ɑ/ before /z/, /a/ before /v ʒ r/.

(40) DISTRIBUTION OF /a/ AND /ɑ/ BEFORE LENGTHENING CONSONANTS IN SF

(a) / __ z

/ɑ/: phrase
     vase
     base
     gaz
     phase

(b) / __ r

/a/: quart
     phare
     renard
     lard
     rare

(c) / __ v

/a/: cave
     lave
     esclave
     épave
     brave

(d) / __ ʒ

/a/: page
     image
     sage
     otage
     gage

What, then, is the situation in CF? It seems, on the one hand, that there exists greater variability in CF, and a general tendency for many of the lengthened occurrences of /a/ to back to /ɑ/ and to be realized as [ɑː], merging thereby with allophones of /ɑ/ and becoming eligible for diphthongization. Let us consider the four lengthening contexts /z r v ʒ/ in turn. That of /z/ is most straightforward, since we have seen in (40) that in SF we find /ɑ/ to the exclusion of /a/ almost without exception in this case, as we do in CF. Phonetically, however, we find in CF a lengthened and diphthongized realization of the vowel before /z/, as illustrated in (41).

(41) phrase   [frɑwz]
      base   [bɑwz]
      gaz   [gɑwz]
      rase   [rɑwz]
      écrase   [ekrɑwz]

Since diphthongization is primarily found in stressed syllables, pretonic occurrences of /ɑ/, even in the same root, will remain monophthongal, although they may still be long: *raser* /rɑze – rɑːze/, *écraser* /ekrɑze – ekrɑːze/.

Before word-final /r/, in addition, CF presents a strong preference for the back vowel /ɑ/, unlike SF, where /a/ predominates. We could see this as a generalization of the CF Backing rule (37), applying to stressed /a/ before /r/. The backed (and diphthongized) versus non-backed variants, depending again on stress, are found in (42).

(42) [ɑw] < /ɑ/   [a] < /a/

   tard   *tardif*
   part   *partir*
   retard   *retarder*
   regard   *regarder*
   art   *artiste*
   part   *partie*

Note, moreover, that the diphthongal variant [ɑw] for /ɑ/ is obligatory (or nearly so) in this case.

Much the same situation obtains before /ʒ/. Recall that SF had extremely few occurrences of /ɑ/ in this context. CF, on the contrary, allows /ɑ/ to occur freely in this position (as in *âge*, *âgé* /ɑʒ, ɑʒe/), and also shows an incipient tendency, strongest in substandard speech, for underlying /a/ to undergo the backing rule. Consider the forms in (43).

(43) [ɑw – aː]   [a]

   nage   *nager*
   image   *imaginer*
   fromage *fromagé*
   garage   *garagiste*
   voyage   *voyager*

Unlike the case with /r/, however, application of the rules of backing and diphthongization preceding /ʒ/ (and /v/ to follow) is optional, and we may find forms such as [naːʒ] *nage*, [imaːʒ] *image*, with [aː] in variation with [ɑw]. Forms involving backing before /v/, of which there are fewer and in which the rule is also optional, are found in (44). (Note that forms like *cadavre, havre, hâve*, which only have [ɑw] and never [aː], are interpreted as containing underlying /ɑ/, parallel to *âge*. Since their vowel is already back, they are not candidates for the process of backing in question.)

(44)
[ɑw – aː]	[a]
cave	caverne
grave	agraver
lave	laver
esclave	esclavage
brave	bravement

In summary, then, the neutralization of the opposition /a/ – /ɑ/ appears to manifest the following pattern in CF: still active, in fact reinforced by the difference [æ] – [ɑw] in closed non-lengthening syllables, the distinction is on the way to being neutralized to /ɑ/ in final open syllables and in lengthened syllables. The phonetic manifestations of the opposition may vary from [ɑ] to [ɔ] word finally, and usually involve the diphthong [ɑw] in lengthening contexts. Thus, the Backing rule (37) above may be extended to apply in the latter contexts, as in (45).

(45) BACKING (REVISED)

$$\begin{bmatrix} V \\ +\text{low} \\ +\text{stress} \end{bmatrix} \rightarrow [+\text{back}] \ / \ \underline{\ \ } \left\{ \begin{matrix} \# \\ \begin{bmatrix} C \\ +\text{lengthening} \end{bmatrix} \end{matrix} \right.$$

Condition: obligatory for the contexts / __ #, z, r; optional preceding ʒ v.

Low vowels become back in final open syllables or before lengthening consonants.

Needless to say, once a vowel is backed by (45), it becomes the input to the normal processes of lengthening and diphthongization which in turn serve to account for the differing surface manifestations. The fact that there remain a certain number of exceptions to the rule (*sage*), that restructurings have occurred (*âge, cadavre*), and that the rule applies in a hierarchical fashion (obligatory / __ z r; optional / __ ʒ v/), all indicate that backing is a typically variable process. It interacts in an interesting way with a process affecting /ɛ/, which is the subject of the next section.

3.7 The lowering of /ɛ/

In absolute word-final position in CF, the lower-mid vowel /ɛ/ undergoes a lowering process, showing up as the low front segment [æ] and, in extreme cases, even as [a]. Consider the forms in (46), where related items demonstrate the presence of underlying /ɛ/.

(46)

laid	[læ]	*laide*	[lɛd]
frais	[fræ]	*fraîche*	[frɛʃ]
prêt	[præ]	*prête*	[prɛt]
parfait	[parfæ]	*parfaite*	[parfɛt]
épais	[epæ]	*épaisse*	[epɛs]
mauvais	[movæ]	*mauvaise*	[movɛ:z]
français	[frãsæ]	*française*	[frãsɛ:z]
lait	[læ]	*laitier*	[lɛtˢje]
paix	[pæ]	*paisible*	[pɛzIb]
craie	[kræ]	*crayon*	[krejɔ̃]
met	[mæ]	*mettre*	[mɛt]
fais	[fæ]	*faire*	[fɛ:r]
plaît	[plæ]	*plaire/plaisir*	[plɛ:r – plezi:r]
vrai	[vræ]		
jamais	[ʒamæ]		

In addition, the endings of the imperfect and conditional singular (*-ais/ait*) furnish a large number of realizations of lowered /ɛ/: *je pourrais* [ʃpuræ], *il était* [jetæ] and so on.

In those cases where the lowered vowel takes on the value [a], it is clear that it must not undergo further backing to [ɑ] or [ɔ]. That is, the rule (45) (Backing) must not apply to produce forms like *[frɑ], *[parfɑ] for *frais* and *parfait*. This problem has engendered a certain amount of theoretical discussion (see, for example, Picard 1978), particularly involving questions of rule order and the blocking of a rule's application. In terms of the present discussion, we may simply say that the phoneme /ɛ/ may have allophones ranging from [ɛ] to [a], while /a/ may vary from [æ] to [ɑ]. But the allophones do not occur in the same contexts: /ɛ/ goes to [a] in open syllables, while /a/ usually backs in those contexts (merging with /ɑ/). In closed syllables, on the other hand, /ɛ/ remains stable, while /a/ is realized as fronted [æ], or else remains invariant. As a consequence, there is no danger of confusion, given that the variation or overlap takes place in mutually exclusive contexts.

From another point of view, the lowering of /ɛ/ represents part of an interesting type of phonological process known as a chain shift—the tendency for related segments to shift in concert, while maintaining their distinctness from each other. Consider the behaviour of the low vowels /ɛ a ɑ/ in final open syllables, against the background of the schema in (47).

(47)   CHAIN SHIFT IN FINAL OPEN SYLLABLES

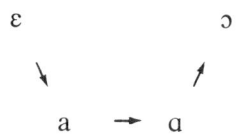

$$\begin{array}{ccc} \varepsilon & & \mathsf{ɔ} \\ \searrow & & \nearrow \\ a & \rightarrow & \mathsf{ɑ} \end{array}$$

We see here a tendency for the lower vowels to rotate counter-clockwise around the periphery of the vowel space. /ɛ/ lowers to [æ] and even to [a] (see (46)), while /a/ backs and merges with /ɑ/ (see (36, 42–44)), where as a result it can, like underlying /ɑ/, be realized as [ɔ]. Recall that this shift takes place only in stressed and *open* syllables, a fact which allows further clarification of the mechanisms involved.

To begin with, the phoneme /ɔ/ never occurs word finally in open syllables in French; there is consequently no danger of a merger between /ɔ/ and /ɑ/ if /ɑ/ were to shift one of its allophones to occupy that space.[10] The /a/ - /ɑ/ distinction does merge here, however, but the role of that opposition is not nearly as important in open as in closed syllables, since very few pairs of words show an /a/ - /ɑ/ difference in absolute word-final position (/ __ #). In closed final syllables (__ C₁ #), on the other hand, no merger takes place at all when the following consonant is a non-lengthening one: *patte* versus *pâte*, etc. Before lengthening consonants, we saw in (42) that there was no real contrast between /a/ and /ɑ/ in any case. /ɑ/ occurs primarily before /z/, /a/ before /v ʒ r/. Thus, whatever happens in the lengthening environment does not cause a significant merger, since neither in SF nor in CF do we find more than a handful of pairs with both /a/ and /ɑ/ preceding the same consonant. Finally, there is no danger of an /ɛ/ - /a/ merger, because the space occupied by /a/ has already been vacated by the backing of /ɑ/. It thus appears that there are internal structural pressures regulating the behaviour of the lower-mid and low vowels in CF, as the chart in (48) makes clear:

---

10. Nor, with one exception, is there danger of an /ɑ/ - /ɔ/ merger in closed syllables. Before non-lengthening consonants, /ɔ/ remains stable; while /ɑ/, being intrinsically long, diphthongizes in CF: *botte* versus *pâte*. In lengthening contexts, we have seen that /ɔ/ does not diphthongize before /v/ or /ʒ/, and it does not occur before /z/; only /o/ is found there. The non-diphthongal quality of /ɔ/ keeps it neatly distinct from /ɑ/ in this position. The only difficulty arises preceding /r/, where /ɑ/ is diphthongized along with /ɔ/ and, predictably, we find the possibility of mergers: *part* and *port*, *quart* and *corps*, *tard* and *tort*, etc. may be homophonous.

(48) REALIZATIONS OF THE CF CHAIN-SHIFTING VOWELS

	__ #	non-lengthening __ consonant	lengthening __ consonant
/ɛ/	a	ɛ	ɛː
/a/	ɑ → ɔ	æ	aː *
/ɑ/	ɔ	ɑw	ɑw *
/ɔ/	(absent from this context)	ɔ	ɔw

*/a/ and /ɑ/ are very nearly in complementary distribution before lengthening consonants; see discussion in text.

As the chart in (48) indicates, even though the four vowel phonemes /ɛ a ɑ ɔ/ may on occasion have identical allophones, they do so in different contexts (with the exception of /a/ and /ɑ/, which merge in the context __ #, cf. column 1). As a result, the phonemes remain distinct, and the chain shift operates only in final position. (See Walker 1983 for more discussion of this shift.)

3.8 *The diphthong* oi

The diphthong *oi* (/wa/ or /wɑ/ in SF) presents some of the most characteristic and complicated behaviour in CF phonology. Remarked on as early as the 19th century (Squair 1888), the variation in *oi* has been often seen as a demonstration of certain archaic phonological properties of CF (by Geoffrion 1934, for example, or Picard 1974b). While these questions are of undoubted interest, we will consider the behaviour of *oi* from a synchronic point of view, outlining first the various realizations of the diphthong. (Here, as elsewhere, it is clear we are dealing with colloquial speech—the greater the attention paid to "correct" pronunciation, the closer will CF approximate the standard. Just as important, however, is the variability—individual, social, regional—that accompanies the phenomenon. Thus, while not all speakers may speak a (popular) dialect identical to the one outlined here, the diversity of the sources consulted assures that the general tendencies outlined are representative.)

At least the following variants of *oi* may be observed: /we wɛ wɛ: wæ wɔ waj wej ɛ e ɔ/. (We will use a phonemic notation /we, wɛ/, etc., even though there will not be phonemic contrasts among all of these variants in any individual dialect.) These alternates are illustrated in (49).

(49) REALIZATIONS OF *oi* IN CF

	(a) /we/	(b) /wɔ/	(c) /wɛ/	(d) /wɛ:/
stressed	*moi*	*pois*	*poil*	*boîte*
	toi	*poids*	*étoile*	*poivre*
	doit	*trois*	*bouette*	*noir*
	boit	*bois*	*moine*	*poile*
	quoi	*mois*	*noisette*	*soir*
	vois	*nois*	*avoine*	*coiffe*
	foi	*loi*	*doivent*	*avoir*
		Dubois	*boivent*	
unstressed	*vois-tu*	*Boisvert*	*soigner*	*coiffé*
	voiture		*voilier*	*poisson*
	moyen		*voyons*	*soirée*
	toilette		*moineau*	*poireau*
	choisi		*coiffer*	*poivré*
	boisson		*boiter*	

	(e) /wæ/	(f) /waj/	(g) /wej/
stressed	*toit*	*noir*	*boire*
	aux abois	*soir*	*poire*
	émoi	*voir*	*noir*
	une oie	*avoir*	*poivre*
	croix	*poêle*	*patinoire*
	doigt	*boîte*	
		coiffe	
unstressed		*soirée*	*déboîter*
		poireau	*poivré*
		coiffé	

THE VOWEL SYSTEM OF STANDARD FRENCH 89

	(h) /ɛ/	(i) /e/	(j) /ɔ/ (especially after labials)
stressed	*droit* *adroit* *étroit* *froid* *à l'endroit*	*crois* (*accroire*)	*poigne*
unstressed		*froidir, -eur* *noyer* *croyable* *nettoyer* *côtoyer*	*poigner, -ée* *-ard, -et* *moitié* *témoigner, -age* *voyons* *moyen(ne)* *poitrine* *loyer* *mademoiselle*

In spite of the diversity of forms presented, we must first note that not every possible realization of *oi* in CF is listed. There are cases of pretonic /wɔ/ (*boisson, choisi*), for example, or of long /ɛː/ (*croire, accroire*) which we have not included because of their rarity or their peripheral status. Much of the remaining material exhibits behaviour that we have already discussed in part. That discussion, particularly from sections 3.1, 3.3, 3.6, 3.7, will help us to systematize the great majority of the developments in (49). It seems clear, that is, that the major realizations of *oi*, /we wɛ wæ wɔ/, behave much like the simple vowels /e ɛ a ɑ/ in CF.

Perhaps the most straightforward cases are those in (h-j) involving /e ɛ ɔ/. Here the diphthong is simplified, and we are left with /ɔ/ as the simplified realization of CF /wa wɑ/. Such adjustments are well known from casual speech, where, for example, we may see deletion of post-stress vowels in English (*sep*ȧ*rate, ref*ėr*ence, mem*ȯ*ry*). Languages may even "institutionalize" these alternations along geographic or social lines: compare the varying realizations of "long ū" in English as /ju/ or /u/ in *due, new, Tuesday*, etc. In the /e – ɛ/ case, moreover, the reduced variants are distributed neatly according to syllable structure: /ɛ/ in closed syllables (49h), /e/ in open (49i), and these pronunciations, though marked as stylistic or geographic (rural, rustic) variations, are phonologically regular. We may characterize them in theoretical terms as undergoing a minor rule of deletion, w → ø / C __ [V, –high] and the detailed phonetic realizations following deletion are described by CF processes already discussed.

The *oi*-variants with the /w/-glide are somewhat more complicated on the surface, but it is possible to discern an underlying regularity, once the variation of the simple vowels in (36) and (46–48) above is considered. In (47), for example, we saw that in word-final position /a/ and /ɑ/ often merged in /ɑ/, which itself had a tendency to back further to [ɔ]. The small set of forms in (49b), a list that is virtually complete, with the exception of a few proper nouns or compounds formed on the basis of items listed, may easily be analyzed as containing underlying /wɑ/, with the variation between [wɑ] and [wɔ] reflecting that of /ɑ/ in final position with which we are already familiar. The forms in /we/ are also few in number. The monosyllables are interesting because many of them enter into minimal pairs with /wæ/ (or even triplets with /wɔ/), and it is easy to suspect semantic pressures at work here helping to maintain a distinction between, say *toi, toit, trois* or *moi, mois*, reinforced by the frequency and the importance of the disjunctive pronouns, which are the most striking members of the /we/ class. Recognition of underlying /we/ in these forms remains one of the major traits distinguishing CF from other dialects in the *oi*-domain. (Forms with pretonic /we/, rare in any case, will not be further considered, particularly since they may all vary with one of the other *oi*-forms.)

It is clear, however, that the greatest number, as well as the greatest diversity of forms, is found in groups (c–g). Yet here again, there appears to be an underlying system compatible with the processes we have already seen. To begin with, the forms in /æ/ (49e) may be considered to realize underlying /wɛ/, since we have already seen in Section 3.7 that in final open syllables, /ɛ/ is pronounced [æ] or even [a]. There is, therefore, a clear similarity between (c) and (e): the former contains /(w)ɛ/ in closed or pretonic syllables, where no lowering occurs; the latter contains the lowered variants of /ɛ/ in stressed final position. What about the forms in (d), where long vowels occur? On the one hand, certain of these vowels are conditioned by the standard lengthening consonants, particularly /r/. However, we also find [wɛː] preceding /f/ and /t/, among others. Here, we may have recourse to the widespread and active CF distinction between /ɛ/ and /ɛː/ (*bêle*: *belle*, *maître*: *mettre*) etc. of (1c) of this chapter, considering contrast to occur between /wɛ/ and /wɛː/ in exactly parallel fashion. Again, parallel to the /ɛ/ - /ɛː/ distinction, there is pretonic variation between long and short vowels, determined in part by the maintenance of a long pretonic vowel when the root is long (*coiffé* based on *coiffe* /kwɛːf/, *soirée* on *soir* /swɛːr/ and so on). Finally, we are left with the diphthongal forms in (f-g). Again, the behaviour of /wɛ/ parallels that of /ɛ/, which we saw in section 3.3 to have diphthongal variants ranging from /ej/ through /ɛj/ to /aj/. Thus, in several domains, including lowering of /wɛ/ to [wæ], presence of a contrast between /wɛ/ and /wɛː/, variation between long and short /wɛ/ in pretonic position, and range of diphthongized variants, /wɛ/ behaves like /ɛ/ in CF.[11]

In summary, the data of (49) may be taken as representing the CF system given in (50) for *oi*-diphthongs:

(50) (a) /we/ – restricted to a few forms, often pronouns (49a).
    (b) /wɑ/ – again highly restricted, realized as [wɔ], parallel to /ɑ/, in final position (49b).
    (c) /wɛ/ – realized as [wɛ] in closed syllables, [wæ] in final position, [wɛː] in lengthening contexts, or [wej-wɛj-waj] when diphthongized (49c-g).

---

11. Note the difference between this analysis and that of Picard 1974b, who analyzes [wæ] as an alternate of /wa/ rather than /wɛ/.

(d) /wɛː/ – in contrast with /wɛ/ in a few forms (*boîte*, *coiffe*) and subject to the same diphthongal variation (49d).

(e) /w/ → ∅ – a minor rule simplifying the *oi*-diphthong in a few marked forms (49h–j), which appear to contain predominantly consonant-liquid clusters preceding the *oi*.

Finally, we should note that the preceding analysis, by considering /wɛ/ as the major representative of the *oi*-diphthong, emphasizes the phonologically archaic character of CF in this respect. We may now turn to the nasalized vowels which present a further domain, of more recent vintage, where CF has not followed the innovative pattern of SF.

3.9   *Nasalized vowels*

We saw in the discussion of SF phonology (Chapter 2) that the standard colloquial dialect contains three nasalized vowels: /ɛ̃ ɑ̃ ɔ̃/, realized phonetically as [æ̃ ɑ̃ õ]. (The vowels /ɛ̃/ and /œ̃/ have merged to /ɛ̃/.) In addition, the nasalized vowels, being members of the class of intrinsically long vowels, are lengthened in stressed closed syllables (*feinte*, *honte*, etc.).

In CF, the situation is markedly different. On the one hand, the Canadian variant has not witnessed the merger of the two front vowels, and is conservative in that respect. On the other, the phonetic realizations of the four nasalized vowels are significantly distinct from those of SF. Compare this phonemic sub-system with its phonetic realizations, as given in (51).

(51) CF NASALIZED VOWELS

(a) *phonemic nasal vowels in CF*

$\tilde{\varepsilon}$ $\tilde{œ}$ $\tilde{ɔ}$
     $\tilde{a}$

(b) *phonetic (short vs long and diphthongized) realizations in CF*

$\tilde{e} - \tilde{\varepsilon}j$ $\tilde{œ} - \tilde{œ}ɥ$ $\tilde{ɔ} - \tilde{ɔ}w$
         $\tilde{æ} - \tilde{a}w$

(c) *examples*

/$\tilde{\varepsilon}$/		/$\tilde{ɔ}$/	
bain	[$\tilde{\varepsilon}$]	bon	[$\tilde{ɔ}$]
cinq		crayon	
faim		rond	
main		gonfle	[$\tilde{ɔ}$w]
quinze	[$\tilde{\varepsilon}$j]	honte	
simple		rompe	

/$\tilde{œ}$/		/$\tilde{a}$/	
parfum	[$\tilde{œ}$]	absent	[$\tilde{æ}$]
un		banc	
défunte	[$\tilde{œ}ɥ$]	gant	
emprunter		banque	[$\tilde{a}$w]
jungle		il vente	
lundi		trempe	

We may first note that the diphthongized long vowels behave like their oral counterparts in terms of the off-glides which they take, and also in terms of a variable (but infrequent) extension of diphthongization to pretonic position (*bonté* [bɔ̃wte], *comprends* [kɔ̃wprɑ̃] etc.). In addition, the non-diphthongized vowels, significantly different in timbre from their SF counterparts ([ẽ æ̃ ɔ̃] in

CF versus [æ̃ ɑ̃ õ] in SF), present a second example of a chain shift such as we saw in connection with the low oral vowels. This time, however, the CF vowel sub-system appears to have rotated frontwards, as (52) indicates.

(52) NASALIZED VOWEL SUB-SYSTEM (PHONETICS)

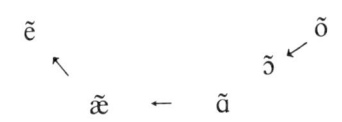

$$\tilde{e} \nwarrow \qquad \tilde{ɔ} \swarrow \tilde{o}$$
$$\tilde{æ} \leftarrow \tilde{ɑ}$$

Thus, while the phonemic inventory and structural relations among the nasal vowels are very similar in SF and CF, the phonetic implementation of the CF system again serves to set off the Canadian dialect in a distinctive manner.

3.10   *Schwa in CF*

Problems involving schwa (*e-muet*, *e-caduc*) are among the most complex and most intensively studied in all of French phonology. We will by no means even enumerate the complete set of areas of interest, restricting ourselves to two domains which seem to characterize the popular speech of French Canada,[12] not to mention the colloquial form of many other French dialects. The first involves certain transpositions or insertions of segments; the second, aspects of schwa deletion. Consider the data of (53).

---

12. We will not, for example, explore the question of the precise phonetic nature of schwa, nor its phonemic status. For contrasting views, see Martinet 1969 and Dell 1973. Various studies by Y.-C. Morin (Morin 1974, 1978, 1983) have given us much additional material of relevance to these problems.

(53) (a) with re- regarder   [ərgarde]
                   reculer   [ərküle]
                   redevait   [ərdvɛ]
                   tout le monde remercie   [... ərmɛrsi]
                   qui revient   [kjərvjẽ]

     with le- le garçon   [əlgarsõ]
               le monsieur   [əlməsjø]
               le nez   [əlne]
               le gardien   [əlgard^{Z}jẽ]

               mercredi   [mɛrkərd^{Z}i]
               brouette   [bərwɛt – barwɛt]
               bretelles   [bərtɛl]
               brebis   [bərbi]
               Frenette   [fərnɛt]

(b) février   [fevərje]   (c) cette   [stə – st]
    clouer   [kəlwe]   cet oeuf-là [ətœflɑ]
    truelle   [tərɥɛl]   de là   [dədla]
    truie   [tərɥi]   de çà   [dədsa]
    truite   [tərɥIt]   de loin   [dədlwẽ] (rare)
    tablier   [tabəlje]
    ouvrier   [uvərje]
    sucrier   [sükərje]
    rien   [ərjẽ]
    voudriez-vous [vudərjevu]

The heterogeneity of this data indicates the complexity of the problem (or problems) involved. Nevertheless, there are certain general tendencies which emerge when the transposition or the insertion of schwa is examined more closely. The two most important are consideration of syllable structure and the general influence of phonotactic patterns involving glides and liquids. Note first that transposition (technically termed metathesis) with *re-* and *le* is favoured if the preceding word in the sequence ends in a consonant, so that the output of the various processes has the general form /(C)əLC/ (where C = consonant, L = liquid and G = glide). There are also word-internal realizations of this pattern, where /CLəC/ passes to /CəLC/ (*brebis, Frenette, mercredi*).

Many of the cases of insertion of schwa (53b) also involve /CL/ clusters—in this case /CLV/ clusters where under normal circumstances the /V/ would have a tendency to become a glide (*scie* /si/ – *scier* /sje/, *tue* /tü/ – *tuer* /tɥe/, where /i/ and /ü/ have become /j/ and /ɥ/, etc.). However, there is a constraint in French blocking (most) */CLG/ sequences, so *plie* /pli/ does not alternate with */plje/, etc. If schwa is inserted before the liquids, however, glide formation may then take place normally: /CLV/ → /CəLGV/: *ouvrier* /uvrie/ → /uvərje/ and so on for the other items of (53b). This principle is at work in certain aspects of French verb morphology, particularly conditional forms: *acheterions* /aʃetrijɔ̃/ alternating with /aʃetərjɔ̃/ etc. (see Morin 1978). Both metathesis and glide formation lead to a significant difference in the occurrence of schwa in CF as opposed to SF. Schwa may not occur in closed syllables in SF, whereas in CF it is frequent in that position: *revient* /ər-vjɛ̃/, *brebis* /bər-bi/, *le nez* /əl-ne/, *tablier* /ta-bəl-je/ and so on. Finally, it is evident that the forms of (53c) are to be separated from the conditions of (53a-b). Considerations of textual frequency, of emphasis, or of morphological structure are much more likely to be involved in this latter, more limited set of items. In *cet* and *cette*, for example, the underlying form may contain schwa rather than /ɛ/: /sət/, /sətə/. In this case, the first schwa of any phrase would be deleted by normal processes, the second (if any) retained: *c∅ livre, c∅t homme, c∅tte femme*; /sliv/, /stɔm/, /stəfam/ respectively.

We have come nowhere near a complete discussion of this type of behaviour in popular French. Nonetheless, the general role of sequential constraints, particularly those involving consonant-liquid sequences, in influencing metathesis or insertion of schwa is clearly evident. Let us now turn to certain differences between SF and CF in matters of schwa deletion.[13]

---

13. Here again, the discussion of schwa deletion will be extremely brief. See Dell 1973 for an extended discussion. The CF material in this section is drawn almost exclusively from Picard 1974a.

Deletion of schwa in SF is governed by a mass of phonological, syntactic, lexical, stylistic and geographic constraints that make any brief synthesis virtually impossible. In this section we will simply note certain ways in which CF may differ from the patterns of SF. Firstly, CF, like the wide range of colloquial French dialects, makes use of a greater frequency and extent of deletion. In phrase-initial position, for example, there is a tendency to maintain a schwa in many of the monosyllable clitics of SF. CF, on the other hand, deletes widely, as illustrated in (54).

(54) *jè vise*
jè te lè donne
què fais-tu
mè vois-tu
cè qu'on voit
lè maître
lè nôtre

Secondly, except for the definite article *le*, which unexpectedly remains unaltered, CF schwa deletion is not blocked by a preceding consonant in the context VC#Cə#C, unlike SF. Picard 1974a gives the examples in (55).

(55) *par le chemin*
car jè prends
Luc sè promène
peur dè rentrer
à part dè cè que jè t'ai dit
peut què jè te fasse mal

Finally, there is a most interesting difference between CF and SF in the type of schwa deletion allowed in adjacent syllables. In many SF sequences, either the first or the second of two mute-*e* may drop, but not both, as shown in (56).

(56)   *jɇ le veux*
                              je lɇ veux
                              *jɇ lɇ veux
                              rɇtenir
                              retɇnir
                              *rɇtɇnir

In CF, to the contrary, only the second drops in sequences of monosyllables (*je lɇ veux*, not **jɇ le veux*); while in polysyllables, the first but not the second is deleted (*rɇtenir*, not **retɇnir*) (Picard 1974a:6). Should this constraint prove systematic in longer sequences (much work remains to be done in this area), the CF data will be of considerable use in resolving certain theoretical controversies, not only in outlining an infrequent type of difference between dialects.

3.11   *Residual problems*

The preceding sections have outlined the major systematic properties of the CF vowel system, against the background provided by "le français général." We have come nowhere near exhausting the set of properties one could investigate: epenthesis of vowels other than schwa (b*a*rouette); substitution of /u/ for /o/ (*arrousoir, routir, routi, pourcelaine*), and so on. We will go no further with this listing, since the phenomena involved are sporadic or of insufficiently wide distribution to characterize CF as a whole. Instead, let us consider one last property of CF, the opening of /ɛ/ to /a/ before /r/ followed by a consonant, which is often considered rural, archaic or otherwise stylistically marked. However, in addition to its wide occurrence in Montreal, and the *outaouais*, it is sufficiently well known to constitute a further trait of the dialect:

(57)   *aubarge*   (*auberge*)
            avarse   (*averse*)
            ciarge   (*cierge*)
            darnière   (*dernière*)
            marci   (*merci*)
            pardu   (*perdu*)
            sarcle   (*cercle*)
            tabarnouche (*tabernacle*)
            viarge   (*vierge*)

In fact, Nyrop 1930:261 noted that such forms in [ar] "constitue[nt] l'un des idiotismes canadiens les plus caractéristiques." Rather than continuing discussion of such irregular or infrequent attributes, let us turn to a summary of the structure of the CF vowel system.

3.12   *Summary and conclusions*

In what follows, we will provide a general picture of the structure of the CF vowel system by setting out two types of summary: initially, of the various rules discussed up to this point, with illustrative examples; second, by giving tables of the principal allophones of the CF vowels, along with the rules that account for them. First, consider the phonological rules applying to CF vowels. (In the case of optional rules, we will assume that the rule has applied in the example given.)

(58)   PHONOLOGICAL RULES—VOWELS

    (a) *Lengthening* (obligatory):
       (i) The vowels /e ø o ɑ/ as well as all nasalized vowels are long in final closed syllables.
       (ii) All vowels are long in final syllables closed by the consonants /v z ʒ r/.
       (iii) Pretonic vowels may be variably lengthened in open syllables: *saute, pâte, honte*; *vire, rêve, part*; *maison, comprend, jeudi*.

(b) *Laxing* (obligatory): The high vowels /i ü u/ are laxed to [I Ü U] in final closed syllables when the consonant closing the syllable is not one of the lengthening consonants: *fils, jupe, coupe.*

(c) *Pretonic laxing* (optional): Pretonic high vowels in closed syllables lax to [I Ü U]: *filtrer purement, roulement.*

(d) *Laxing harmony* (optional): Pretonic high vowels in open syllables lax to [I Ü U], particularly if a syllable to the right contains a lax high vowel: *ministre, pupitre, cousine.*

(e) *Diphthongization* (obligatory): Stressed long vowels take diphthongal off-glides agreeing with the vowel nucleus in frontness and rounding (the rule may be optionally extended to pretonic long vowels): *père, trempe, pâte.*

(f) *Vowel devoicing* (optional): High vowels in medial syllables devoice when preceded and followed by voiceless obstruents: *équiper, occuper, écouter.*

(g) *Vowel deletion* (optional): Vowels may be deleted in the first or second syllable of a word, primarily when the vowel is high and the context contains fricatives or sonorants: *professeur, politique, piscine.*

(h) *Backing* (optional): The vowel /a/ backs to /ɑ/ in final open syllables and before lengthening consonants (there are additional constraints on backing in the second context, where backing also creates segments which undergo diphthongization): *chat, éclat, écrase, quart.*

(i) *Lowering* (obligatory): The vowel /ɛ/ lowers to [æ] in word final open syllables: *jamais, frais, parfait.*
Note that *Backing* and *Lowering* also apply to condition certain realizations of the diphthong *oi*: *trois, bois* with /ɔ/; *toit, doigt* with [æ], etc.

(j) *W-deletion* (optional, minor): The diphthong *oi* is simplified by dropping the /w/ in certain forms: *voyons, droit ("drette"), froid ("frette").*

(k) *Lowering before* /r/ (optional, minor): /ɛ/ lowers to /a/ in certain forms before /r/ + C: *merci, dernière, averse.*

THE VOWEL SYSTEM OF STANDARD FRENCH 101

This concludes the list of rules which are active in producing distinctive pronunciations in CF. Of these rules, lengthening in final syllables is characteristic of all dialects of French. Laxing, Diphthongization (for Montreal, at least) and Backing are all obligatory, and constitute a key part of the definition of CF. Devoicing, Pretonic laxing, and the extension of long vowels or diphthongs to pretonic position are all widespread, and carry little if any social marking (they are not perceived as sub-standard speech). Lowering of /ɛ/ to /a/, either in final position or before /r/, pronunciations of *moi* or *toi* as /mwe/, /twe/, certain variants of *oi* other than /wa/, backing and diphthongization of /a/ to /ɑ/ or /ɑw/ pretonically or before /ʒ/, on the other hand, are less widespread and are considered "poor" speech (*joual*, under certain definitions of that term). We will give similar classifications—inherently CF, widespread and socially unmarked, stigmatized—when we discuss consonants in the next chapter. Before that, however, let us summarize certain stable allophones in the vowel system, allophones produced by the rules of (58), in the tabulation of (59).

(59) PRINCIPAL VOWEL ALLOPHONES IN CF

    (a) *High vowels* /i ü u/

        [I Ü U]   – laxing, laxing harmony, pretonic laxing
        [iː yː uː] – lengthening
        [Ij Üɥ uw]– diphthongization
        [i̥ y̥ u̥]   – devoicing
        Ø   – deletion

    (b) *Higher-mid vowels* /e ø o/

        [eː øː oː] – lengthening
        [ej øɥ ow] – diphthongization

(c) *Lower-mid vowels /ɛ (ɛ:) œ ɔ/*

[ɛ:(ɛ:) œ: ɔ:] – lengthening
[aj aj œɥ ɔw] – diphthongization
[æ – a] – lowering of /ɛ/
[a] – lowering of /ɛ/ before /r/

(d) *Low vowels /a ɑ/*

[æ] – realization of /a/ in closed stressed syllables
[ɑ – ɔ] – backing of /a/ in final open or lengthening syllables
[ɑw – ɔw] – diphthongization (of both /ɑ/ and /a/ when backed)

(e) *Nasalized vowels /ɛ̃ œ̃ ɔ̃ ɑ̃/*

[ẽ œ̃ ɔ̃ ɑ̃] – general shift of CF nasalized vowels
[ẽ: œ̃: ɔ̃: ɑ̃:] – lengthening
[ẽj œ̃ɥ ɔ̃w ɑ̃w] – diphthongization

Even in this summary, we have excluded a certain amount of information. The standard context for the high and higher-mid vowels, for example, is that of final open syllables, where there is no deviation from the underlying norms of /i ü u e ø o/. For the lower-mid vowels, syllables closed by non-lengthening consonants provide the least variable environment, as we can see in the forms *cette, seul, sotte* [sɛt sœl sɔt]. The rest of the vowels are less homogeneous in their behaviour. Nor have we, moreover, given a full set of variants for certain segments: [ɑ] is often in free variation with [ɔ], for example, and the richness of the diphthongal realizations of /ɛ/ and /ɑ/ is great.

We have, nevertheless, been able to outline a considerable diversity of CF vowels. It is fair to say that CF presents a particularly rich area of study, both in its underlying inventory of vowels and in the complex and interesting variety of phonetic realizations of this system. Full exploitation of this mass of data has only just begun; its relevance for further phonological studies should be evident.

Further Reading—Canadian French Vowel System

Few general surveys of the CF vowel system are to be found. Much relevant material occurs in the works by Gendron 1966a, Juneau 1972 and Santerre 1976b already mentioned in the list for Chapter 1, as well as in Dulong and Bergeron 1980. The rest of the references will be organized according to the specific topic in question.

Length; diphthongization: Baligand and James (1979)
Dumas (1974b, 1978, 1981)
Santerre and Milo (1978)
Laxing: Dumas (1976, 1978, 1981)
Légaré (1978)
Devoicing: Gendron (1959)
Deletion: Jacques (1974)
Santerre (1975)
Low Vowels: Bossé and Dugas (1983)
Picard (1978)
Santerre (1974, 1976b, c, d)
Sturm (1932)
oi: Geoffrion (1934)
Picard (1974b)
Nasalized vowels: Charbonneau (1971)
Poulin (1973)
Schwa: Lafollette (1960)
Picard (1974a)

CHAPTER 4

The Canadian French Consonant System

4.0   *Introduction*

We have already seen that the French consonant system, including that of CF, is less rich and less typologically complex than the corresponding vowel inventory. Summarized again in (1), the consonant system is simple and straightforward.

(1)   FRENCH CONSONANTS, BOTH CF AND SF

p	t		k	
b	d		g	
f	s	ʃ		
v	z	ʒ		
m	n	ɲ	ŋ	
	l			r

In terms of divergence from SF, CF consonants also present fewer contrasts than do its vowels. Most of the differences, moreover, will lie less in the area of allophones than in the morphophonemic domain—particularly the presence or absence of segments or sequences of segments. There is, however, one major allophonic property of CF that sets it apart from SF, a property that is highly characteristic of the dialect.

4.1   *Assibilation*

Assibilation is a process whereby sounds, particularly stops, become strident (with an "*s*-colouring"). In the case of CF, the apical stops /t d/ become the affricates [t^s d^z] when followed by a high front vowel or glide, as in (2).

(2)   ASSIBILATION OF /t d/

[tˢ]	[dᶻ]
tigre	diner
type	dire
petit	indigne
attirer	crocodile
tube	dur
tunnel	dupe
coutume	rendu
battu	pendule
tiens	indien
tiède	diète
tuer	conduire
tuile	duel

This assibilation, a type of assimilation that falls within the general domain of palatalization, is well known from historical and comparative studies. What is particularly interesting in the CF case is the way that assibilation is conditioned by aspects of grammatical structure, notably the presence or absence of word boundaries, and the role of compound word and clitic constructions. Basically, the constraint seems to be that assibilation takes place only within words, not across word boundaries. But when clitics or compound words are involved, assibilation can occur between the separate morphemes, although without the obligatory status of the word-internal process. Consider the data in (3), which are representative of one major sub-dialect. (Other types of behaviour involving assibilation also occur.)

(3) WORD BOUNDARIES AND ASSIBILATION

    (a) *parfait idiot*   [t], [d] only
        petit Yvon
        voute immense
        grande histoire
        vite irrité

    (b) *Sept-Îles*   [t] or [t^s], [d] or [d^z]
        (compare *sept îles* with only   [t])
        avant-hier

    (c) *part-il*   [t] or [t^s], [d] or [d^z]
        parle-t-il
        pas d'idée
        d'images
        (compare *dix mages* with only   [d^z])
        d'huile
        je t'y retrouverai

In the case of (3a), we will consider that two # boundaries are present, reflecting the "strength" of the disjunction between the two formatives. In (3b-c), however, only a single boundary occurs, consistent with general principles of phonological theory (see Selkirk 1972, for example) and this weaker link permits assibilation. The rule of assibilation, then, contains an optional word boundary, and is formulated as in (4).

(4) ASSIBILATION

$$\begin{bmatrix} C \\ +\text{ant} \\ +\text{cor} \\ -\text{cont} \end{bmatrix} \rightarrow \begin{bmatrix} +\text{delayed} \\ \text{release} \end{bmatrix} / \_\_ (\#) \begin{bmatrix} -\text{cons} \\ +\text{high} \\ -\text{back} \end{bmatrix}$$

/t/ and /d/ become the corresponding apical affricates when they precede high front vowels or glides.

CF is not, in fact, completely homogeneous in its behaviour with respect to assibilation. For certain speakers, assibilation is obligatory within words (including compounds and clitics) but optional between two "full" words. For such speakers [pt^{s}it^{s}ivɔ̃] *petit Yvon* is a possible pronunciation. There are still consistent differences between intra- and inter-word contexts, however, reflected in the obligatory versus optional application of the rule in the two positions. Still other speakers assibilate everywhere, except with nouns preceding adjectives or with *d'* + V. Historically speaking, it appears that assibilation started within words (a context to which it is still limited in conservative dialects) and is gradually spreading to all environments regardless of intervening boundaries or type of construction. But whatever the ultimate outcome, it is clear that the process remains the major allophonic consonantal modification characterizing CF. Other features have more to do with insertion or deletion of segments, as we shall see.

4.2   *Final consonant deletion*

SF has an optional rule simplifying final consonant-liquid clusters, and also deleting two stops in certain masculine-feminine adjective pairs or derived forms:

(5)   (a) *la tabl̸e̸*
            le sabl̸e̸
            le prêtr̸e̸
            l'ancr̸e̸

            (b) *distin̸c̸t̸*   —   *distincte*
                exa̸c̸t̸   —   *exacte*
                instin̸c̸t̸   —   *instinctif*
                aspe̸c̸t̸   —   *aspectuel*
                respe̸c̸t̸   —   *respectueux*

CF shares this tendency and has carried it forward to a greater degree than is found even in colloquial SF. One could suggest that CF is moving toward a stage where no final consonant clusters except those of the form LC (liquid-consonant) will be permitted. The forms in (6) reflect this tendency, although it is clear that full regularization of word-final clusters to the LC# pattern has not yet been obtained. In particular, the sequence /ks/ or, more generally, /Cs/ is acceptable in word-final position: *mixte, sexe, prétexte*, etc. The same applies to certain occurrences of /sk/, as in the forms *puisque, lorsque, jusque* (compare *disque, grotesque, juste*). The status of /s/ in phonotactic constraints has always involved the possibility of various types of exceptional behaviour. In particular, these forms will have to be excluded from the domain of application of consonant deletion ((7) below).

(6)   FINAL CONSONANT DELETION

    (a) -CL#

aveuglé	*perdŕé*
cerclé	*peuplé*
coffŕé	*pourpŕé*
contŕé	*probablé*
convaincŕé	*propŕé*
défendŕé	*rompŕé*
entŕé	*simplé*
équilibŕé	*soufflé*
faisablé	*tabernaclé*
filtŕé	*tablé*
manoeuvŕé	*vinaigŕé*
miraclé	*vivŕé*
octobŕé	*votŕé*

(b) -sCL#

minis̸t̸r̸e̸
mus̸c̸l̸e̸
orches̸t̸r̸e̸
pias̸t̸r̸e̸
semes̸t̸r̸e̸

(c) -CC#

abrup̸t̸	*concep̸t̸*
ac̸t̸e̸	*correc̸t̸* (very frequent)
adep̸t̸e̸	*intac̸t̸*
à la pos̸t̸e̸	*jus̸t̸e̸*
à l'es̸t̸	*mix̸t̸e̸*
anglicis̸m̸e̸	*oues̸t̸*
architec̸t̸e̸	*péquis̸t̸e̸*
ça res̸t̸e̸ comme ça	*prétex̸t̸e̸*
catéchis̸m̸e̸	*ryth̸m̸e̸*
collec̸t̸e̸	*socialis̸m̸e̸*

It is clear that word-final position (and, consequently, syllable-final position) is a weak one for consonants. Deletion in this position, therefore, is perfectly in accord with general tendencies of phonological behaviour. As to the formalization of the process, the rule in (7) represents an initial effort.

(7) FINAL CONSONANT DELETION

$$C \rightarrow \emptyset \;\; / \begin{bmatrix} C \\ -son \end{bmatrix} \_ \#$$

Delete word-final consonants when they follow a non-sonorant consonant.

This rule must be allowed to delete two consonants in those cases where a word ends in a group of three consonantal segments (*ministre, piastre*, etc.) The precise formal means of assuring this do not concern us here. We will turn instead to a converse process, the extension or insertion of certain consonants in word-final position in CF.

4.3   *Final consonant retention or insertion*

Here again, we are dealing with a phenomenon that is already familiar from the standard language, illustrated in (8), where several forms show alternates with a final consonant that has been retained or, on occasion, inserted (sometimes for morphological or semantic reasons):

(8) EXTENSION OF FINAL CONSONANTS IN SF

but	[büt]
ananas	[ananas]
plus	[plüs]
fait	[fɛt]
août	[ut]

Again characteristic of CF is the extent to which the process has spread (or, on occasion, where CF has retained final consonants that may fluctuate in SF, as in *ananas, but, août*). For CF, we may note two main areas: forms parallel to the SF examples, and proper nouns. Note that it is /t/ which is almost exclusively present in final position.

(9) FINAL /t/ IN CF

    (a) *bout*   [bUt]
        juillet   [ʒɥijɛt]
        bleuet ("beluette")   [bəlɥɛt]
        inquiet   [ɛ̃kjɛt]
        adroit   [adrɛt]
        ticket   [tˢikɛt]
        debout   [dəbUt]
        pas du tout ("pantoute")   [pãtUt]
        tout à fait   [tUtafɛt]
        ici   [isIt]
        prêt   [prɛt]
        pourrie   [purIt]
        crue   [krÜt]
        laid   [lɛt]
        nuit   [nɥIt]
        lit   [lIt]
        froid ("frette")   [frɛt]
        complet   [kɔ̃plɛt]

    (b) *Brunet*   -all with final /t/
        Morisset
        Chabot
        Pouliot
        Ouellet
        Ouimet
        Talbot
        Vinet
        Boutet

    This process calls for several comments. First, it manifests a tendency to create closed syllables, a phenomenon which contradicts the oft-quoted preference of French for open syllabification. It is relevant to note, however, that ever since the increased frequency of schwa deletion, SF itself has seen the creation of more and more closed syllables: /vi-tə/ → /vit/ *vite*, /kɔ̃-plɛ-tə-mã/ → /kɔ̃-plɛt-mã/ *complètement*, and so on. The movement toward open syllables can no longer be taken to be as strong as it once was in French, standard or otherwise. (In this respect, see also Encrevé 1983.) This trend is even less evident in CF, given further processes such as gemination, resyllabification involving schwa (see section 3.10), or the retention/insertion of final /t/ that characterize Canadian speech.

Secondly, there appear to be various motivating factors in this increased presence of final consonants. The support of the orthography is evident, as is the preponderance of /t/ as the final consonant. The fact that /t/ occurs is no doubt linked to its important role in liaison (*grand homme* /grɑ̃tɔm/), as a feminine signal (*petit – petite* /pti – ptit/), and as a signal of third person in verbs forms (*vient-il* /vjɛ̃til/). Finally, the frequency of the phenomenon in proper names is striking—there is a tendency to generalize it to all names in -Vt#, although the underlying pressures for this remain to be elucidated.

4.4   *Nasal assimilation*

We saw in the discussion of colloquial SF that there was a tendency for voiced stops to assimilate to either a preceding or a following nasal segment (vowel or consonant), thereby passing to the corresponding nasal: /b-m, d-n, g-ŋ/, as in *bombe* /bɔ̃m/, *dinde* /dɛ̃n/, *dingue* /dɛ̃ŋ/. This process is very widespread (although still variable) in CF, and is reflected in the examples in (10).

(10)   (a) *ensemble*   /ɑ̃sɑ̃m/
            septembre   /sɛptɑ̃m/
            novembre   /nɔvɑ̃m/
            ombre   /ɔ̃m/
                               (compare *homme* /ɔm/)
            épingle   /epɛ̃ŋ/
            ongle   /ɔ̃ŋ/
            jungle   /ʒœ̃ŋ/
            langue   /lɑ̃ŋ/
            blonde   /blɔ̃n/
            grande   /grɑ̃n/
            lendemain   /lɑ̃nmɛ̃/

(b) une heure et demie /... enmi/
aide-mémoire /ɛnmemwar/
diagnostique /djaŋnɔstik/
redemander /rənmɑ̃de/
admirer /anmire/
froidement /frwanmɑ̃/
solidement /sɔlinmɑ̃/
enjambement /ɑ̃ʒɑ̃mmɑ̃/
fragment /fraŋmɑ̃/
vaguement /vaŋmɑ̃/
longuement /lɔ̃ŋmɑ̃/

These examples are interesting in a number of ways. Note first that nasalization (assimilation) of the voiced stops occurs following nasalized vowels, as well as preceding nasal consonants. This process also provides examples violating the constraint against nasalized vowels preceding nasal consonants in French (*/VN/). Except in certain rare and morphologically determined contexts (notably the prefix en/em: emmagasiner, emmener, etc.), such sequences are not normally found outside popular speech. However, the fact that innovations can produce new phonetic sequences violating this constraint (ensemble /ɑ̃sɑ̃m/, grande /grɑ̃n/) indicates that the phonotactic system, the system governing constraints on sequences of sounds, is undergoing modifications that may ultimately result in more far-reaching structural change.

Finally, we should note that nasal assimilation reinforces the status of the velar nasal [ŋ] in French. Excluded from the standard phonemic inventory, [ŋ] is found in a number of loan words (parking, training, smoking and so on) of somewhat marginal status. However, the presence of these loans, the added creation of allophonic [ŋ] via assimilation (épingle [epɛ̃ŋ], longue [lɔ̃ŋ] etc.), plus the natural place a velar nasal finds in the series /b-m, d-n, g-ŋ/ all indicate that the SF system is ready for the recognition of a new phoneme. In the CF context, this introduction is reinforced by a further process, to which we now turn.

4.5   *Velarization of /ɲ/*

The palatal nasal /ɲ/ in CF is subject to a variety of pressures, one of which is the exchange with /nj/ to which we alluded in the second chapter. The second major force, however, involves the backing of that segment to the velar nasal [ŋ] whenever /ɲ/ is in syllable-final position. Consider the data in (11):

(11)   [ɲ]   [ɲ]   [ŋ]

   baigner   *baigne*   *baignoire*
   signer   *signe*
   enseigner   *enseigne*   *enseignement*
   vignoble   *vigne*
   peigner   *peigne*   *peignoir*
   gagner   *gagne*   *gagne-pain*
   ligner   *ligne*   *enlignement*
                 champagne
                 compagne

Here, we see that when /ɲ/ occurs preconsonantally or in word-final position, that is to say at the end of a syllable, a productive process causes it to be realized as the velar [ŋ]. This rule, which makes crucial use of the notion of syllable boundary, is given in (12).

(12)   VELARIZATION OF /ɲ/ (OBLIGATORY)

$$\begin{bmatrix} C \\ +\text{nasal} \\ -\text{anterior} \end{bmatrix} \rightarrow [-\text{coronal}] \ / \_\$$$

Palatal /ɲ/ is realized as [ŋ] in syllable-final position.

It appears that, in structural terms, this velarization process is sufficient to argue for the creation of a new nasal phoneme in CF, since there is no way to distinguish the [ŋ] in *enseignement*, where the source is /ɲ/, from that in *longuement*, where the [ŋ] results from the nasalization of /g/. Both words, moreover, must also be distinguished in this area from *pleinement* with /-nm/ as opposed to /-ŋm/, or *amnésie*, with /-mn/, and so on.

4.6 The phoneme /r/

Let us now turn to the pronunciation of *r* in CF. Like its continental relative, CF has a single *r*-phoneme, but the allophones of the CF segment vary even within a small area. Writing in 1970, Vinay noted that the majority of Canadian speakers have an apical trill, [r̃], but that an important sub-group, centred around Quebec City, realizes /r/ as a uvular sound [R]. This latter usage is expanding. In a more localized and more detailed study, Santerre 1978 examines the status of /r/ in Montreal on the basis of the Sankoff-Cedergren corpus. Santerre demonstrates the active presence of both [r̃] and [R] in Montreal, adding a number of interesting precisions to the work of Vinay. Most important is the fact that the apical sound predominates among older speakers, but that the younger generations (under 35) have [R] in a proportion of almost 3 to 1. It is also evident in Santerre's study that women have a greater proportion of [R] than do men, and that [R] also takes on greater importance in more formal speech situations. Each of these factors—age, sex and style—is well known from other socio-linguistically oriented research, and the general profile of the distribution of [R] confirms the expansion of that allophone to which Vinay alluded. The behaviour of the realizations of /r/ in general conforms directly to the constraints on variable rules which we have already seen to be functioning in various vocalic domains.

4.7 Residual or restricted phenomena

In this section we will examine a number of phenomena of restricted geographic distribution or infrequent occurrence. Such items are however sufficiently characteristic of CF to warrant passing mention.

4.7.1 *h*

No phoneme /h/ occurs in SF, the designation "aspirate-h" referring to a type of lexically conditioned irregular behaviour (lack of elision or liaison, selection of irregular allomorphs) rather than to a phonological segment. In CF, on the other hand, a phonetically present [h] may be heard in a restricted number of forms (and more extensively under emphasis). Such forms may either be indigenous, usually representing "aspirate-h" forms in SF, or English loans. It appears, moreover, that many pronunciations with *h* are often hypercorrections, characteristic of upwardly mobile speakers and of women.

(13) *h* IN CF (WORDS REALIZED WITH [h] FOR ORTHOGRAPHIC *h*)

haut	/ho/
haïr	/hair/
hache	/haʃ/
hardi	/hardi/
harnais/harnois	/harnɛ/
dehors	/dəhɔr/
hâler	/hale/
harpe	/harp/
hose	/hoz/

4.7.2 *Mellowing*

A further phenomenon, characteristic of but by no means limited to the Beauce region in Quebec (it is frequently heard in unguarded speech in the Ottawa-Hull region, for example), involves the mellowing of the consonants /ʃ/ and /ʒ/ to a voiceless and voiced *h* respectively (which we will note [x] and [H]). Many authors have seen fit to comment on the process (Vinay 1970, Hull 1966, for example), and Léon 1967 has studied the links between the Canadian variants and the dialectal sources, notably Norman, in France. The words in (14) are representative; the notation is that of Léon 1967, which has found wide currency in CF linguistics.

(14) [x] AND [H]

chercher	[xarxe]	geler	[Həle]
hache	[hax]	neiger	[neHe]
cheval	[xəval]	jambe	[Hã̆m]
chaud	[xo]	jupe	[HÜp]
ruche	[rÜx]	gentil	[Hãnt^s i]

Note that both [x] and [H] remain distinct from the [h] of *haut* or *hache*; consequently for this sub-dialect it is necessary to recognize a three-way contrast /h/: /x/: /H/.

4.7.3 Loss of /r/ and /l/

Liquids are, in a sense, weak consonants, and are widely lost both historically and dialectally in a variety of contexts in French. Various examples of their deletion in CF are found in (15), where the predominance of syllable-final position is evident.

(15)

	arbre	/ab/
	-eur	/-ø/
	mercredi	/mɛkrədi/
	oublier	/ubije/
	parce que	/paskə/
	parle	/pal/
	plus	/pü/
	plutôt	/püto/
	quelque	/kek/
	sur le bord	/sülbɔr/
	trois	/twa/

These examples are only a small set of those showing loss of /r/ or /l/, and are typical of popular speech in all French dialects, not just CF. Nor have we indicated the loss of /l/ in certain clitics—articles and pronouns—which, along with the gemination of /l/, will occupy us in a later chapter. Finally, in the

THE CANADIAN FRENCH CONSONANT SYSTEM 119

more general context, we have omitted discussion of the assimilation of voicing in consonant clusters, either obstruent-sonorant or obstruent-obstruent sequences. Very little distinguishes CF from SF in this domain, but the one factor that does occur has taken on particular importance in the linguistic folklore of Quebec. In SF in word-initial clusters of fricatives, the voiced consonant assimilates to the voiceless, whatever their relative position: *je fais* /ʃfe/, *cheval* /ʃfal/, and so on. In CF, on the other hand, the first consonant, so it is claimed, assimilates to the second, so that *cheval* is realized as /ʒval/ which passes to /ʒwal/, written *joual*. This is the reputed origin of the term often used to represent popular or rural speech, a term that has become highly visible and controversial in the CF context. Clearly, however, few if any speakers pronounce all initial clusters in this way, and the word *joual* has a rural origin, despite its frequency (or notoriety). Because of the phonological structure of French, very few other potential examples of this type of assimilation exist; *cheville* /ʒwij/ and *cheveu* /ʒwø/ are two that have been cited in addition to *joual*. We see, then, that a process does not have to be widely applicable in order to have major impact on the linguistic consciousness of a community.

4.8   *Summary and conclusions*

We may now, in a fashion parallel to that of the preceding chapter, summarize the major processes affecting consonants.

(16)   CF CONSONANTAL MODIFICATIONS

(a) *Assibilation* (obligatory): The apical stops /t/ and /d/ become [tˢ] and [dᶻ] preceding high front vowels and glides: *tire, dur, tiens, duel*.

(b) *Final consonant deletion* (optional, frequent): Final consonant clusters are simplified to the form V(L)C # (with /s/ having an exceptional status): *probablé, octobŕé, cerclé, perdŕé, ministŕé, piastŕé, communisté, ouesť, adepť, intacť, mixťé* (/miks/), *prétexťé* (/preteks/).

(c) *Final consonant insertion* (variable, obligatory in certain words): Final /t/ is realized in word-final position: *bout, juillet, debout, pas du tout* (/pãtut/), *ici* (/isit/), *prêt, cru* (/krüt/), *Morisset, Talbot*. (Rather than an exclusive rule of insertion, it may often be preferable to speak of retention of final consonants in this case, with the choice of insertion or retention depending on the word in question.)

(d) *Nasal assimilation* (optional): Voiced stops adjacent to nasal segments (vowels or consonants) become the corresponding nasal: *ensemble, grande, longue, rapidement, longuement*.

(e) *Velarization of* /ɲ/ (obligatory): The palatal nasal /ɲ/ becomes /ŋ/ in syllable-final position: *signe, ligne, enseignement*.

We have eliminated from this list those phenomena which are either unsystematic or are restricted in scope (mellowing, liquid deletion). Even were they to be included, the contrast between the CF vowel and consonant systems is remarkable: the former presents enormous differences from SF; the latter very few, and most of those are rooted in popular aspects of continental varieties of pronunciation. There is one set of consonantal alternations involving /l/ deletion and gemination in the clitic system which remains highly characteristic of CF. We will return to that domain in the final chapter after brief consideration of the prosodic system of CF. First, however, let us note, as we did with the vowels (see section 3.12), the status of certain processes affecting consonants. To begin with, assibilation (4.1) is obligatory; one cannot be a speaker of CF without it. Final consonant deletion (4.2), insertion of /t/ in proper nouns (4.3), and the deletion of /l/ (see Chapter 6 below) are widespread and unremarkable in social terms. Other final consonants, as in *icitte, drette* (*droit*) and so on, again characterize "joual". But it remains clear that it is the vowel system of CF that provides the bulk of the distinctive properties of Canadian speech. Study of the prosodic domain will provide no reason to modify this claim.

FURTHER READING—CANADIAN FRENCH CONSONANT SYSTEM

General survey: Hull (1966)

Assibilation: Charbonneau and Jacques (1972)
        Haden (1941)
        Rousseau (1940)

Final consonants: Kemp, Pupier and Yaeger (1980)
        Pupier and Drapeau (1973)
        Pupier and Grou (1974)

/r/: Clermont and Cedergren (1979)
    Santerre (1979, 1982)
    Vinay (1950)

Mellowing: Charbonneau (1957)
        Hull (1960)
        Léon (1967)

CHAPTER 5

The Prosodic Structure of Canadian French

5.0　*Introduction*

There is no absolute agreement in phonological circles as to what phenomena may properly be considered as falling within the prosodic domain. Most generally, prosody is considered to include anything not specifically involved in the articulation of individual segments. Thus, aspects of syllable structure, rhythm, duration, stress, tone, intonation, speech rate, and even pauses have all been considered as prosodic at one time or another. What seems to link these cases together, in addition to their tendency to go beyond the bounds of single segments and to be linked to the syllable, is their contrastive or relative nature. One speaks of relatively high or low tone, greater or lesser duration, stronger or weaker accent and so on.

　　For a variety of reasons (but definitely not including lack of intrinsic interest or linguistic relevance), much prosodic terrain has remained relatively unexplored, both in general terms and in the CF domain. Recently, however, much of the work emanating from the Phonetics Laboratory of the University of Toronto (Léon et al. 1970) is helping to remedy this situation. In this chapter, we will survey briefly the "core" prosodic areas of length, stress, tone and intonation as they pertain to Canadian French.

5.1.　*Length*

We have already surveyed in some detail the distribution of long vowels in CF. On the one hand, the distribution parallels that in SF, in that long vowels are found in closed final syllables preceding /v z ʒ r/; or, in the case of tense or nasal vowels, in any closed final syllable (see section 3.2). On the other hand, CF does present certain clear differences from SF: the /a/: /ɑ/ and the /ɛ/: /ɛː/ distinctions are much more widespread and stable; the long vowels are often diphthongized under stress and in marked contrast with lax, short variants and so on. But perhaps the main difference from SF (though far less so in the case of colloquial varieties; see, for example, Mettas 1979) is in the extension or the maintenance of the occurrence of long vowels in pretonic (usually penultimate) position:[1]

(1) b*u*reau   [bü:ro]
     d*a*nser   [dɑ̃:se]
     éc*oeu*rer   [ekœ:re]
     enc*a*drer   [ɑ̃kɑ:dre]
     il est f*â*ché   [jefɑ:ʃe]
     je c*o*mprends   [ʃkɔ̃:prɑ̃]
     la m*aî*trise   [lame:tri:z]
     l*i*rer   [li:re]
     se p*â*mer   [spɑ:me]

Differences of length may affect consonants as well as vowels, and long consonants are well known in SF in a number of contexts:

(2) LONG CONSONANTS IN SF

     (a) between words
         ce*tte t*able   /tt/
         une cou*pe p*olie   /pp/
         la gro*sse s*ouche   /ss/
     (b) following deletion of schwa word-internally
         honnê*tet*é   /tt/
         troisiè*mem*ent   /mm/
         teintu*rer*ie   /rr/

---

1. Both colloquial European French and SF show considerable numbers of pretonic long vowels. There remain differences between the dialects, however, in both the vowels undergoing lengthening and in the contexts for the process. Much further work is needed before any systematic conclusions may be drawn.

(c) in learned words
    gra*mm*aire   /mm/
    i*nn*é   /nn/
    co*ll*ègue   /ll/
    i*mm*ense   /mm/
    i*ll*égal   /ll/
    co*mm*entaire   /mm/
    i*nn*ombrable   /nn/
    i*rr*égulier   /rr/

(d) under the "accent d'insistance"
    c'est *t*errible   /tt/
    quel *c*atastrophe! /kk/
    im*p*ossible   /pp/

(e) in various restricted morphological contexts
    je cou*rr*ai, mou*rr*ai /rr/
    i*l l*'a vu   /ll/
    je *ne n*ie pas que... /nn/

Each of these types of geminate consonant is also found in CF, although with differing degrees of frequency. In addition, however, CF has developed a further set of morphologically conditioned geminates, again linked to analogous developments in colloquial French, that enlarge the number and type of long consonants in CF, and modify the morphological system in an interesting way. Examples are given in (3).

(3)   *je l'ai vu*   [ʒəllevü]
           tu l'as vu   [tˢüllavü]
           il en a   [innɑ]
           vous en avez   [vunnave]

We will consider this CF type of variation in much greater detail in the chapter dealing with morphophonemics and the morphology of pronouns. In any case, it is clear that CF has innovated, with respect to SF, in both consonantal and vocalic length, and that these innovations have implications for the stress system.

5.2 Stress

"Stress" refers, in phonological terms, to the degree of prominence given to a syllable in comparison with its surrounding syllables. One speaks of stressed or unstressed syllables, and it is possible to distinguish varying degrees of stress. In SF, the final syllable of the word is stressed; and within larger phonological phrases, this word stress is subordinated to a phrase-final or pre-pausal stress. Stress placement in SF, as a result, is predictable and non-distinctive, serving a demarcative function (indicating word or phrase-final syllables, as the case may be).

The notion of stress is a complex one, referring normally to a perceptual difference. The physical parameters influencing this perception include intensity (amplitude), frequency and duration. While all three appear to influence stress perception, the relative importance of each of them varies from language to language. In French, for example, the factor that most influences the perception of stress is length: long syllables are clearly perceived as more stressed than short ones. At the same time increased intensity and higher frequency also play a role, albeit of lesser importance. In other words, stressed syllables in French are longer, louder and of higher pitch than unstressed ones, but it is their greater length that is most significant in determining their being perceived as stressed.

Thus, questions of vowel length in French are not independent of stress. In SF, the fact that long vowels are restricted to final closed syllables will obviously help to reinforce the perception of those syllables as accented, if their vowels are long. However, if long vowels start to appear in non-final position in popular speech or in Canadian French, these long vowels will also cause changes in the perception of stress. As a consequence, we also find stress occurring in these varieties on non-final syllables, those which have been lengthened. Consider the examples in (4).

(4)   co*n*tent   [kɔ̃́:tã]
        *e*n tout cas   [ã́:tukɑ]
        il va n*ei*ger   [ivané:ʒe]
        c'est-tu têtu   [setˢüté:tˢü]
        ce*n*t piastres [sã́:pjas]

This extension of non-final lengthening/stress shift appears to be expanding in (colloquial varieties of) SF and is clearly evident in CF.

The reasons for this CF growth in the number of items with non-final stress are obscure. We may note, however, that the expansion parallels an increased use in the "accent d'insistance" noted, among others, by Fouché (1956:lxii):

> L'accent d'insistance devient fréquent, si fréquent qu'il peut paraître normal.... Le langage de la société cultivée maintient l'accent sur la finale. Mais pendant combien de temps le français familier résistera-t-il à la poussée du français populaire? Et une fois le français familier atteint, qu'adviendra-t-il du français plus soigné?

It is not impossible, then, that the greater frequency of the "accent d'insistance" on non-final syllables in popular spoken French is linked with the stress shift to non-final syllables in CF, reinforcing the tendency to lengthen the vowels in those syllables.

Such speculations raise further questions, however, such as the nature of the relationship between stress and length. Does the stress shift to non-final vowels, which then become long, or do these vowels first lengthen and provoke a differing interpretation of stress placement? Whatever the answer to such questions, which involve a broad range of factors, it is clear that the links between stress and vowel length in spoken French are close and complex. The same may be said for the connection between these two factors and that of rhythm.

Rhythmic patterns involve the interplay between prominent and non-prominent syllables, whether prominence involves length, stress, or a combination of both. The SF pattern is said to be that of a syllable-timed language, where each syllable in the phonological phrase, except the last, is of roughly equal duration and prominence, producing the typical "staccato" rhythm of standard French. In CF, on the other hand, the modifications in the distribution of length and stress will clearly produce a different rhythmic pattern. The degree of difference from SF is variable (and debatable). We will give the last word on this subject to Boudreault, whose work on spoken French remains of prime importance in analyses of this question (even if his study appears to underestimate the differences between the two varieties):

> notre travail nous amène à la conclusion qu'il n'existe pas de différences essentielles de rythme et de mélodie entre le français parlé au Canada et le français parlé en France.... La durée relativement longue de la prétonique chez les Canadiens paraîtrait le trait le plus caractéristique pouvant entraîner une différence de quelque importance dans le rythme de la langue des deux communautés, si le phénomène pouvait être considéré comme un déplacement d'accent, s'il se produisait régulièrement et seulement chez eux.... Tous ces particularismes que nous avons relevés n'entraînent pas chez les Canadiens un rythme et une mélodie étrangères à la langue française. (Boudreault 1968:120–122).

5.3   *Tone*

Tone refers to the perceived pitch on individual syllables, pitch being largely a function of the rate of vibration of the vocal cords. Tone languages are those which make distinctive use of tone differences, and may be divided into two major types: those where the pitch is constant during the entire syllable, and those where the tone changes "direction", either rising or falling. We thus speak of level versus contour tones.[2] Strictly speaking, therefore, French, including CF, is not a tone language, since it does not use tone differences to distinguish morphemes. There do occur, however, two marginal phenomena that may properly be included in the tonal domain. The first involves a rising-falling tone pattern, expressive in nature, that may accompany lengthened pretonic

---

2. There has been a recent explosion in the attention devoted to questions of tone (see Fromkin 1978, for example). We can give only the barest summary here, ignoring in particular questions of the morphophonemics of tone and tonal patterns over longer sequences.

vowels in emotional speech (in particular, in several of the "jurons" that are frequent in colloquial speech). Such contours may furnish a kind of hyper-characterization of the "accent d'insistance":

(5) câlice   /kâːlis/
     câline   /kâːlin/
     c'est assez drôle ça   /... drôːl.../
     content   /kɔ̂ːtɑ̃/
     je comprends   /ʃkɔ̂ːprɑ̃/
     pas du tout   /pâːtut/
     tabernacle   /tâːbarnak/

As we have seen, there are both stylistic and lexical restrictions on this type of tonal phenomenon, which remains highly limited. The second type of tonal patterning is somewhat more systematic, and involves specific contours that arise on vowel sequences across syntactic boundaries. It has been investigated in ground-breaking work, by Santerre and Ostiguy 1978 as well as Santerre and Villa 1979, who demonstrate that the frequency changes are but one of a series of effects (including intensity, duration, assimilation, fusion and so on) that distinguish major from minor junctures and preserve certain phonetic indications of grammatical structure. The following examples are taken from Santerre's work (note that " ∧ " indicates a rising-falling pattern, and "—" a level tone):

(6) pâte à pain   /pɑwtapẽ/
     pas # où t'as peint /pɑ̂wtapẽ/
     tu peux # (ne) pas en faire davantage
     tu (ne) peux pas # en faire davantage
     pendant tout ce temps-là, on a attendu le messie
     Papa, il trouvait ça écoeurant
     c'était au jugement du gars, le gars, il disait...

These examples, involving contiguous syllables as well as questions of grammatical structure (inter- versus intra-phrasal sequences of vowels), lead naturally into a discussion of intonation.

5.4 Intonation

Intonation involves tonal patterns over longer sequences, usually defined in terms of syntactic phrases. It is necessary to distinguish two types of use of intonation, the first for grammatical purposes, the second for expressive. In grammatical terms, intonation is often used to indicate sentence type, declarative or interrogative, as well as non-final position:

(7)   (a) *vous venez* ⬊
     (b) *vous venez?* ⬈
     (c) *vous viendrez, si vous le pouvez.* ⌒

Secondly, intonation is used, depending on the situation, to indicate a gamut of emotions, a use that leads immediately into the vastly complex area of the expressive function of language and of phonostylistics, an area which is only beginning to be explored with any confidence, and which we cannot treat here.

In the present context, it is worth noting that there is no unanimity of opinion regarding the intonational structure of CF. In part, this diversity may be traced to differences of style in the samples studied (formal – popular, written – spoken) or even to regional differences within Canada (Ontario versus Quebec French[3]). One view sees little difference between SF and CF. Boudreault (1968:121-122), for example, claims, in line with his general approach that results in a de-emphasis on the differences in question, that "Ce schéma mélodique est le même dans les phrases prononcées par les sujets canadiens et français." Boudreault does

---

3. Holder 1972, Maury and Wrenn 1973, and Baligand and James 1973 all study intonation patterns in Ontario French, finding differences in comparison with SF and, on occasion, with aspects of Quebec French.

find, however, a greater range of intra-sentential frequency variation among speakers of SF, distinguishing it from CF. This latter conclusion echoes the preliminary results of Gendron 1966:154-155, who observed that,

> En l'occurrence, le terme "monotone" est un terme qui convient à l'intonation canadienne par rapport à l'intonation parisienne... en fait, ce n'est pas le schéma général de l'intonation qui diffère, dans la phrase affirmative, entre les deux parlers, mais seulement le détail du mouvement tonal: en canadien, l'écart est moindre entre la note la plus basse et la note la plus haute et les modifications de la voix sont aussi moins prononcées. Cet aspect mélodique de la phrase contribue beaucoup, semble-t-il, à donner au parler canadien un caractère particulier en face du français de France.

Against this view, at least partially, we may set the remarks of Delattre 1971:122, who asserted that "Il doit y avoir, dans l'intonation du français au Québec, des courbes caractéristiques qui le distinguent du français de Paris. Ces courbes résonnent dans nos oreilles pendant des semaines après un séjour au Québec." As with many other aspects of prosody, both in general and in French linguistics, a precise determination of these "résonances" remains a task for the future.

FURTHER READING—PROSODY

Much work has recently been undertaken in this area, of which Lehiste 1970 presents a general survey, as do the relevant chapters of Hyman 1975. The CF material is organized under three headings.

Length: Baligand and James (1979)
Stress:　Boudreault (1968, 1970)
　　　　　Yaeger and Kemp (1977)
Tone and intonation: Baligand (1973)
　　　　　　　　　　 Baligand and James (1973)
　　　　　　　　　　 Maury and Wrenn (1973)
　　　　　　　　　　 Santerre and Ostiguy (1978)

CHAPTER 6

Questions of Canadian French Morphophonology

6.0   *Introduction*

"Morphophonology" refers to changes in the phonological shape of morphemes, depending on their segmental or grammatical context. It involves, then, different pronunciations of the same word, and has often been included in grammatical (morphological and lexical) sections rather than in strictly phonological discussions. Before entering into detailed examination of CF morphophonology, it may be useful to outline briefly certain properties which distinguish phonological from morphophonological processes.

Phonological rules (rules which account for allophones or for neutralization) are those which are defined in strictly phonetic terms, without reference to non-phonetic information. Such rules are automatic, non-suppressible and productive (they may interfere with foreign language acquisition, they apply to all new words entering the language and so on). The rules of vowel laxing or assibilation in CF are phonological rules. Such rules may, on occasion, be variable, and subject to social or even to grammatical constraints. However, if the latter *block* rather than condition the rule's applicability, they are not enough to remove it from phonological status. We have had ample opportunity to see variable rules in the preceding chapters.

Morphophonogical rules, on the other hand, are much more restricted. Such rules typically affect subsets of the lexicon or specific morphological categories. They have exceptions, are not usually productive, and often show a tendency to undergo the pressures of analogy. In English, for example, the alternation between voiced and voiceless fricatives in singular-plural or noun-verb pairs (*house-houses, knife-knives*; *breath-breathe, life-live, house*[s]-*house*[z]) is morphophonemic. It occurs in specific grammatical contexts; it is not regular, and it is slowly being eliminated (consider the *Toronto Maple Leafs* (not **Leaves*), for example). In the same way, the vocalic changes in various singular-plural or present-past tense forms (*mouse-mice, goose-geese, bite-bit, ride-rode, sing-sang*, etc.) are morphophonemic. It will be clear in what follows that the morphophonology of CF presents a variety of problems fully equivalent to the complexities of the vowel system we saw in the third chapter.

There remain, however, two questions of detail before these problems can be investigated. First, there is a long-standing debate concerning the role of word boundaries in phonological rules. The traditional (concrete or structuralist) position is that word boundaries may not be included in such rules, although these boundaries may block the application of a rule. (This position reflects a constraint against mixing levels in analysis. Since word boundaries incorporate grammatical information, they may not be used in strictly phonological rules.) Any rule containing # (the symbol for word boundaries) would then automatically become morphophonemic in character. Recent work by Clayton (1981) and others, in contrast, has shown that the distinction between rule types may be made on the basis of a number of independent criteria, and that the presence or absence of word boundaries is irrelevant in determining the status of a rule as phonological or morphophonological. There is a large amount of data in CF bearing on this matter, since we have seen several processes in both the vocalic and consonantal domains that crucially involve #. More importantly, however, both the backing of /a/ and the lowering of /ɛ/ take place only in the *presence* of these boundaries; that is, only in absolute word-final position (see sections 3.6, 3.7). In other respects, however, Assibilation, Lowering and Backing are phonological, not morphophonemic rules. It would appear, therefore, that CF material supports the more supple conclusion that strictly phonological rules may still make reference to the boundaries of words.

Secondly, since morphophonology deals obviously with morphology, both in the classes of items undergoing modification and in the contexts that provoke the changes, we will on occasion refer to morphological notions: pronoun types, clitics, verb stems, analogy and so on. We will also mention, in passing, certain phenomena that are more properly morphological than morphophonological in nature, although no systematic study of CF morphology is possible here. Nevertheless, the close links between morphophonology and morphology proper are of clear relevance to the remarks which follow. Finally, as Morin 1979 makes clear, there are great overlaps between CF and colloquial continental French in the morphophonological domain, and the characteristics of CF discussed below should not be taken as unique to that dialect.

6.1   *Simple pronoun subjects in CF*

Subject pronouns, distinguished for two numbers, three persons and (in the third person only) for two genders, normally accompany finite verbs in French. The SF forms, both orthographic and phonological, are summarized in (1), where the major role of liaison in conditioning variation is evident.

(1)   STANDARD FRENCH SUBJECT PRONOUNS

(a)

	Singular	Plural
1st person	*je* /ʒə ʒ ʃ/	*nous* /nu nuz/
2nd person	*tu* /tü/	*vous* /vu vuz/
3rd person	*il* /il/	*ils* /il ilz/
	elle /ɛl/	*elles* /ɛl ɛlz/
	on /ɔ̃ ɔ̃n/	

(b)

je le vois	/ʒəlvwɑ/
j'entre	/ʒɑ̃tr/
je comprends	/ʃkɔ̃prɑ̃/
on arrive	/ɔ̃nariv/
nous vendons	/nuvɑ̃dɔ̃/
nous arrivons	/nuzarivɔ̃/

The forms in (1) are typical of SF. Colloquial French, including in particular CF, introduces a wide variety of additional modifications, particularly in the second singular and in third person pronouns. *Tu* becomes /t/ before vowels; *il* is uniformly /i/

before consonants and /j/ before vowels. The plural form *ils* is also frequently found with the same allomorphs as singular *il*, even in liaison contexts where one would expect /iz/. As for *elle*, it is normally realized as /a/ before consonants (and, under different circumstances, as /ɛ/ or /al/ before vowels, a situation to be discussed below). The plural *elles* also takes the form /a/ in the same context. Even more striking, moreover, is the frequent disappearance of *elles* in favour of the masculine forms /i-iz/. These variants are tabulated and illustrated in (2).

(2)   (a) *tu*   /t/ __ V
           il   /i/ __ C, /j/ __ V
           ils   /i/ __ C, /iz - j/ __ V
           elle   /a/ __ C, /al - a/ __ V
           elles   /i/ __ C, /j/ __ V

    (b) *tu (n')es pas capable*   /tepakapab/
        tu (n')arrives jamais à temps   /tarivʒamɛ .../
        il va venir   /ivavnir/
        il vient   /ivjɛ̃/
        il est   /je/
        ils vont   /ivɔ̃/
        ils ont   /jɔ̃ - izɔ̃/
        ils arrivent   /jariv - izariv/
        elle vient   /avjɛ̃/
        elle arrive   /alariv - aariv/
        pas qu'elle sache   /pakasaʃ/
        elles vont partir, les filles   /ivɔ̃partir.../
        les filles, elles ont pas pu venir   /lefij jɔ̃papüvnir/

Finally, we may note a restricted phenomenon involving the first singular pronoun *je* preceding *me*. Here, there is a type of assimilation resulting potentially in the complete disappearance of the pronoun, although traces are often left in the form of a lengthened nasal consonant:

(3)   *je m'en vais*   /mmãvɑ/
       je m'en fous   /mmãfu/
       je me demande si...   /mənmãd.../

The preceding remarks have been largely morphophonological in nature. Certain morphological comments are also relevant to an understanding of the pronominal system. As will be apparent from the sample sentences, for example, the negative morpheme *ne* is virtually absent from spoken French. Secondly, the indefinite pronoun *on* is expanding its domain, and has almost completely replaced *nous*, as in *On y va-tu, nous autres?* or *Nous-autres, on est ici*. (*On*, on the other hand, is frequently replaced by *ça*: *ça parle fort par-là*.) Finally, plural pronouns are reinforced by suffixing *-autres* /ot/ to *nous*, *vous*, *eux*, accompanied by repetition of the simple subject:

(4)   *On fait pas ça, nous-autres*
       Vous y allez, vous-autres?
       Eux-autres, ils savent mieux s'expliquer, vous savez.

As is well known, none of these traits is specific to CF. Each characterizes popular spoken French in general, and plays a major role in the morphology of the CF pronominal system.

A maximal set of pronominal distinctions is found in Table (1a) of this chapter. A reduced system, incorporating the variants and innovations discussed above, is given in (5), which will also serve as a starting point for a discussion of object pronouns.

(5)   COLLOQUIAL CF PRONOUNS

	Singular	Plural
1st person	ʒə / __ C ʒ / __ $\begin{cases} V \\ \begin{bmatrix} C \\ +\text{voice} \end{bmatrix} \end{cases}$ ʃ / __ $\begin{bmatrix} C \\ -\text{voice} \end{bmatrix}$ m / __ m (opt.)	ɔ̃(n) nu(z) nuzot
2nd person	tü / __ C t / __ V	vu(z) vuzot
3rd person (a) masc.	i / __ C j / __ V	i / __ C $\left.\begin{matrix} \text{iz} \\ \text{j} \end{matrix}\right\}$ / __ V
(b) fem.	a / __ C al / __ V	$\left.\begin{matrix} \varepsilon \\ i \end{matrix}\right\}$ / __ C $\left.\begin{matrix} \varepsilon l \\ \text{iz} \\ \text{j} \end{matrix}\right\}$ / __ V

6.2   *Direct object pronouns*

There are three direct object pronouns in French: *le, la, les*. The first shows the frequent effects of schwa deletion, and appears with the allomorphs /lə/ and /l/. It also undergoes gemination to /ll/, a phenomenon we will consider in a later section. The remaining pronouns, *la* and *les*, are subject to one of the most interesting and complex processes in CF morphophonology: *l*-deletion, which is illustrated in (6).

(6) DELETION OF /l/ IN OBJECT PRONOUNS

    (a) *la*:
        je la veux   /ʒavø/
        tu la prends-tu   /tüaprãtü – taprãtü/
        je la vois pas   /ʒavwɑpɑ/
        il la prend   /japrã/
        il va la chercher   /ivɑɑʃɛrʃe/

    (b) *les*:
        je les veux   /ʒevø/
        tu les prends-tu   /tüeprãtü – teprãtü/
        je les vois pas   /ʒevwɑpɑ/
        il les prend   /jeprã/
        il va les chercher   /ivɑeʃɛrʃe/
        tu les as eus   /tezaü/

These examples allow us to identify several of the constraints on *l*-deletion in CF. To begin with, deletion is preferentially restricted to the pronouns (and articles) *la* and *les*, and usually when the /l/ is in intervocalic position: the /l/ does not delete in *geler, tulipe, vallée* and so on, even though the phonological context /V __ V/ is identical to those in (6). (Poplack and Walker 1983 discuss the structure of *l*-deletion in CF in much more detail.) Nor does it delete in *pour la voir, Paul les a vus*, /pɔllezavü/, or when the pronoun is accented, as in *prends-la pas, remet-les à Jean*, and so on. This deletion, moreover, gives us information regarding the phonological representation of subject pronouns in CF. Third singular *il*, for example, must have the form /i/ (not /il/) in order to provide an appropriate deletion context, as in (7).

(7)   *il les a vus*   /i # le # z # a # vü/
        l-deletion   ø
        (l → ø)
        glide formation   j
        (V → G/ __ (#)V

                                    /jezavü/

If the representation were /il/, the /l/ of the object pronouns would not be in intervocalic position, and could not delete. Analogous arguments apply to first person *je*, which must be /ʒə/, with a vowel, in order to provide the context for deletion. (Note the alternate pronunciation, not typical of the style in question, for *je les ai vus*: /ʒlezevü/, with schwa deletion but no *l*-deletion.)

There is also an interesting assymetry in the behaviour of pronoun objects: *la* and *les* frequently show deletion, *le* and *l'* (from *le* or *la* elided before vowels) rarely do. There is, in fact, a clear functional explanation of this difference in deletion. When the /l/ deletes in *la* or *les*, the vowel of the pronouns remains (often indirectly, through its effects on the surrounding sounds) to signal the presence of the object markers. But if the *l* from an elided pronoun were to delete (as in *je l'ai vu*), then all trace of the object pronoun would disappear, and the phrase would be homophonous with *j'ai vu*. The case of *le* is slightly more complex. If *le* is represented as /l/, without schwa, then deletion has the same effects as in the case of the elided pronouns—total disappearance of the pronouns. But if *le* is given the representation /lə/, its preceding and following contexts must be considered. These contexts will either engender the dropping of /ə/ (as in *vous l∅ avez vu* or *vous l∅ voyez*), or the dropping of /ə/ in a preceding morpheme (as in *je le regarde* /ʒlərgard/). Thus, whatever happens, the appropriate conditions for *l*-deletion will not be met: either the *l* will not be in an intervocalic position, or here too the deletion would eliminate the pronoun completely. We are presented, therefore, with a clear case of the influence of grammar on phonology—the maintenance of a morphological distinction—with grammatical conditions affecting phonological behaviour. We will return later to the separate treatment of *le*; in the meantime, the examples of (8) illustrate the maintenance of *le* and *l'* in the conditions just discussed.

(8) (a) *je les vois*
/ʒə # le # vwɑ/
    ø   *l*-deletion
    ø   ə-deletion (ə → ø / __ (#) V)
/ʒevwɑ/

(b) *je l'ai vu*
/ʒə # l # e # vü/
   —   *l*-deletion (fails because of
                      the functional constraint)
   ll   gemination (see below)
/ʒəllevü/

(c) *je le vois*
/ʒə # lə # vwɑ/
   ø   ə-deletion
   —   *l*-deletion (fails because /l/
                     is not intervocalic)
/ʒəlvwɑ/

Let us now turn to the behaviour of articles, which parallels in a striking fashion the treatment of pronouns which we have just examined.

6.3   *Articles*

Not surprisingly because of their phonological similarity, the articles in question show behaviour parallel to that of the pronouns *le, la, l', les*. It is interesting to observe, however, that while popular continental French deletes widely in pronouns, loss of *l* in articles appears to represent an innovation limited to CF. This behaviour is illustrated in (9).

(9)   DELETION OF /l/ IN ARTICLES

  (a) ça vaut la peine   /savoapɛn/
    c'est pas la même chose   /sepɑamɛmʃoz/
    j'ai vu la fille   /ʒevüafij/
    Paul a les mains sales   /pɔlɑemɛ̃sal/
    j'ai les pommes puis les oranges /ʒeepɔmpiezɔrɑ̃ʒ/
    je les ai vus, les gars   /ʒezevüegɔ/
  (b) après le souper   /aprɛlsupe/
    j'ai pris le livre   /ʒeprilliv/
    j'ai pas l'habitude   /ʒepɑlabitüd/
  (c) à la maison   /aamezɔ̃/
    devant la maison   /dvɑ̃amezɔ̃/
    sous la table   /suatab/
    durant la nuit   /dürɑ̃anɥi/
    dans les maisons   /dɑ̃emezɔ̃/
    chez les autres   /ʃeezot/
    sans les enfants   /sɑ̃ezɑ̃fɑ̃/
    parmi les gars   /parmiegɔ/

The examples in (9a) show deletion in the articles *la* and *les*, parallel to the object pronouns. (9b) gives examples of *le* and *l'* where no deletion occurs, following the same constraints that occurred in section 6.2. The very productive process of deletion of /l/ after prepositions ending in vowels is illustrated in (9c). (In further cases, examples such as those in (9) may serve as input to additional processes to be discussed below.) Moreover, (9c) allows us to consider three other factors affecting *l*-deletion in articles. The first involves the variability of deletion on the basis of the specific prepositions involved. Certain prepositions, particularly frequent monosyllabic ones, appear to condition *l*-deletion much more easily than others. Deletion after *à*, *dans*, *sur*, for example, is "easier" than after *durant*, *malgré*, *parmi*, although the precise conditions governing this variability remain to be analyzed in detail. It appears, however, that the more frequent the preposition, the more frequent the deletion of *l*.

Prepositions supply the second area of comment as well. Prepositions ending in /r/ (*par, pour, sur*) may on occasion lose this consonant, thereby creating an appropriate context for *l*-deletion. This phenomenon is illustrated in (10).

(10) *il est passé par la porte*   /... paapɔrt/
            par la fenêtre   /paafnajt/
            par les bois   /paebwɑ/
      pour la femme   /puafam/
      pour les élections   /puezelɛksjɔ̃/
      sur la table   /süatab/
      sur les étagères   /süezetaʒajr/

Finally, we have noted that elided *le*, that is *l'*, rarely deletes, neither as an article nor as a pronoun. In fact, however, there are a few occurrences of the article *l'* deleting when followed by /e/ or /ɛ/ in particularly frequent, if not fixed, expressions, especially with feminine nouns:

(11) *devant l'école*   /dvãekɔl/
      à l'église   /aegliz – ajgliz – ejgliz/
      dans l'escalier   /dãɛskalje/
      à l'hôpital   /aɔpital/

This, too, is a variable phenomenon that forms part of the larger network of *l*-deletion in CF, a network that has at its centre the deletion of /l/ in *la* and *les* under specific conditions, and at its periphery an expansion of this deletion process either by creating additional contexts for deletion (loss of /r/ in prepositions) or by violating in minor ways constraints on loss of the liquid (dropping of elided *l'*). But there remain still more complicated pronominal structures and further morphophonemic processes.

6.4   *Complex cases: indirect objects, gemination, fusion, and other processes*

The indirect object pronouns in French are *lui* and *leur*. Both of these are modified in colloquial French in ways that are related to *l*-deletion. Consider the data in (12).

(12)   (a) *lui* and *leur* in CF
       je lui donne   /ʒidɔn/
       tu lui donnes   /tüidɔn/
       il lui donne   /iidɔn/
       on lui donne   /ɔ̃idɔn/
       tu lui as acheté   /tüjɑaʃte/
       elle lui a acheté   /ajɑaʃte/
       elle lui achète   /ajaʃɛt/

       (b) Alongside the regular form /lœr/, we also find /løz/, as well as additional variants:
       je leur ai dit   /ʒløzedi – ʒjøzedi/
       tu leur as dit   /tüløzadi – tüjøzadi/
       il leur donne   /ilødɔn/
       on leur a demandé   /ɔ̃løzɑnmɑ̃de/
       vous leur dites   /vuløditʼ/

These examples indicate that *lui* /lɥi/ may lose both the liquid and the glide in popular speech, reducing to /i/ and then varying between /i/ and /j/ depending on whether a consonant or a vowel follows. In this, it is identical to the behaviour of *il*. The form *leur*, on the other hand, shows greater resistance to the loss of /l/ and considerable variation occurs even within the dialect in question. The general trend seems to be to retain the /l/, while on rare occasions it may become /j/. Two other factors increase the variability of *leur*, the tendency to drop the /r/ preconsonantally, and the widespread insertion of /z/ as a "false" liaison consonant linked to the plurality of the pronoun (*je leurs ai dit* and so on). Finally in this context we may add examples containing two object pronouns, each of which is subject to the innovations of popular speech.

(13)   *on le lui a donné*   /ɔ̃jadɔne/
        il me les a donnés   /imezadɔne/

In this case, however, we are often confronted with a morphological rather than a morphophonemic problem, since there appears to be a constraint such that when the indirect object is in the third person, the direct object pronoun is deleted, as it is in colloquial SF. Thus, the sequences *le, la, les* plus *lui* or *leur* occur simply as *lui* or *leur*: *je le lui ai donné* /ʒjedɔne/ etc. This deletion may be linked to the differing position of indirect object pronouns relative to direct objects. First and second person indirect object pronouns precede *le, la, les*, while *lui* and *leur* follow. Deletion of direct objects preceding *lui* and *leur* in popular French avoids this positional conflict.

     We have, up to this point, been primarily concerned with reduction in the "mass" of the pronouns *le, la, les, lui, leur* through deletion of /l/, accompanied on occasion by other changes. Neither the articles nor the pronouns *le* and *l'* are capable of deleting under normal circumstances. They are, however, subject to a process of reinforcement or gemination, which occurs in all of colloquial French but which is particularly frequent in French Canada. (For a discussion of the origins of this phenomenon, see Paris 1877.) In fact, the general strategy seems to be "if you can't delete, geminate" or perhaps "geminate before deletion gets you", to speak metaphorically. The examples of (14) illustrate the process, which affects *en* as well as *le*.

(14) (a) *je l'ai vu*   /ʒəllevü/
     tu l'as   /tülla/
     il l'a pris   /illapri/
     on l'a pris   /ɔ̃llapri/
     vous l'avez   /vullave/
     je te l'ai donné   /ʒtəlledɔne/
     je l'entends   /ʒəllɑ̃tɑ̃/
     tu l'enverras demain   /tüllɑ̃veradmɛ̃/

  (b) *j'en ai*   /ʒənne – ʒɑ̃ne/
     tu en as   /tünna – tɑ̃na/
     il en a, il y en a   /inna – jɑ̃na/
     elle en a   /anna – alɑ̃na/
     on en a   /ɔ̃nna – ɔ̃nɑ̃na/
     vous en avez   /vunnave – vuzɑ̃nave/
     ils en ont   /innɔ̃ – jɑ̃nɔ̃/
     tu en enlèves   /tünnɑ̃nlɛv – tɑ̃nɑ̃lɛv/
     il en oublie   /innubli – jɑ̃nubli/

The examples of (14) incorporate the variety of changes affecting pronoun subjects (*tu* = /tü/ or /t/; *il/ils* = /i/ or /j/; *elle* = /a/ or /al/ etc.) which we have already seen. As for the pronoun *l'* (but not the article), it regularly occurs as the germinate /ll/ when a vowel follows. The behaviour of *en* is slightly more complex. In prevocalic position, it may present its regular liaison variant /ɑ̃n/. When in intervocalic position, however, it frequently appears in the truncated form /n/, which undergoes the same gemination as the /l/ of *l'*. The results are seen in (14), which contains the last examples dealing specifically with pronoun allomorphs. Let us now turn to certain further consequences of the variation, and in particular the deletion, of /l/ as it affects these forms.

We have, in fact, already seen one of the processes at work in the alternation between /i/ and /j/ for *il/ils* depending on the following segment: /i/ precedes consonants, while /j/ precedes vowels, as in *il donne* /idɔn/ versus *il est* /je/. This phenomenon exemplifies a general French alternation between high vowels and glides (seen in verbal paradigms, for example: *scie-scier* /si/ – /sje/, *joue/jouer* /ʒu/ – /ʒwe/, etc.). In the CF case, *l*-deletion creates new sequences meeting the conditions for glide formation, as in (15).

(15)   *il les attend*   /jezatã/
            les femmes puis les enfants   /lefampjezãfã/
            tous les gars   /twegɔ/
            sous la table   /swatab/
            sur la table   /sɥatab/
            tu lui a parlé   /tüjaparle/
            pour la femme   /pwafam/

While it is normally the initial vowel of a VV sequence which becomes a glide, there do exist a few isolated examples of the second vowel changing to a glide. Such cases, illustrated in (16), must be considered irregular, since the loss of /l/ (from *l'*) is not usual.

(16)   *à l'église*   /ajgliz/
            d'après les filles   /daprɛjfij/

The fact that the new V + V sequences created by the loss of /l/ subsequently undergo glide formation serves to illustrate the productivity of the latter process. If it were not productive, there would be no reason for the high vowels in question to become glides. When the vowels involved are not high, moreover, or if the rule of glide formation does not apply, different changes take place—changes which involve deletion or fusion of vowels.

     CF, as do many languages, appears to have constraints against sequences of vowels. While these constraints are not absolute (hiatus does occur in CF, and frequently), there is clear pressure to reduce VV sequences, either by the aforementioned gliding, or by vowel elision or fusion. (In cases of fusion, the resulting vowel will be different from either of the source vowels.

Elision, on the other hand, implies simple disappearance of one of the vowels, with the second remaining unchanged.) Consider the data in (17).

(17) (a) *Elision*   V → ø / __ V

tu les a eus	/tezaü/	ü – e
il me les a donnés	/imezɑdɔne/	ə – e
il revenait à la campagne	/irəvnɛakɑ̃paŋ/	a – a
il va la changer demain	/ivaʃɑ̃ʒenmɛ̃/	ɑ – a
c'est la musique	/samüzik/	e – a

      (b) *Fusion*   V V → V:

sur la table	/sa:tab/	ü – a
il lui donne	/i:dɔn/	i – i
demande à la soeur de Marie	/... a:sœr.../	a – a
pour changer les lumières	/... ʃɑ̃ʒe:lümjajr/	e – e
dans les bois	/dɛ̃:bwɑ/	ɑ̃ – e
avant la classe	/avɑ̃:klas/	ɑ̃ – a
durant la nuit	/dürɑ̃:nɥi/	ɑ̃ – a
elle les a pris	/ɛ:zɑpri/	a – e
il craint les orages	/ikrɛ̃:zɔraʒ/	ɛ̃ – e
elle est venue	/ɛ:vnü/	a – ɛ

It is not possible to examine in detail the many complexities of this behaviour, which still remains poorly understood. It appears, however, that fusion is more frequent than elision, that distance from the main stress influences the length of fused vowels (*demande à la vieille* /... a:vjej/ contains a longer vowel than *demande à la vieille fille malade*, for example), and that not all vowel sequences are subject to fusion. In particular, if the first vowel of the pair is back or round, there appears to be far less chance of fusion, and a sequence of two vowels remains:

(18) va la chercher   /vaɑʃerʃe/
      ça vaut la peine   /savoapɛn/
      c'est pas la même chose /sepɑamɛmʃoz/
      ils font la grande vie   /ifɔ̃agrɑ̃nvi/
      ils vont la voir   /ivɔ̃avwɛjr/

Finally, we should note that, even where no fusion takes place, there is a strong tendency for nasalized vowels to transfer their nasality to their neighbours; such progressive assimilation, seen in (19), is well known from general phonological studies.

(19) dans la glace   /dɑ̃:glas/   ɑ̃ – a
      dans les meilleurs familles /dɛ̃:mɛjœr.../ ɑ̃ – e
      avant les examens   /avɑ̃ɛ̃zɛgzamɛ̃/ ɑ̃ – e
      ils sont les plus riches   /isɔ̃ɛ̃püriʃ/   ɔ̃ – e

6.5 Summary of rules

Nasal assimilation was the last of the morphophonemic processes to be discussed in this chapter. Let us then recapitulate and exemplify the various phenomena seen up to this point. They will be divided into two categories, morphological and morphophonological, although in the case of certain minor or highly constrained processes, the distinction is a difficult one to maintain with certainty. (If a process is restricted to the specification of suppletive allomorphs of a single morpheme, we will consider it to be morphological in nature.)

(20) MORPHOLOGICAL INNOVATIONS

  (a) *ne* is absent from spoken French: *j'en ai pas, il est pas venu.*

  (b) many subject pronouns have special reduced variants: *tu* /t/, *il/ils* /i/, *elle* /al/ ~ /a/.

  (c) plural *elles* is replaced by *ils* (and consequently, in phonological terms, becomes homophonous with *il*).

(d) *-autres* is frequently added to disjunctive pronouns and used to reinforce a pronoun subject: *les femmes, eux-autres, elles sont bien.*

(e) *lui* is reduced to /i/; *leur* remains /lœr/ or reduces to /lø/ – løz – jø – jøz/: *on lui a donné* /ɔ̃jadɔne/, *je leur ai parlé* /ʒjøzeparle/.

(f) in sequences of direct object pronouns (*le, la, les*) plus indirect objects (*lui, leur*), the direct object pronoun is often deleted: *je le lui ai donné* /ʒjedɔne/.

(g) *en* has the variants /ã/, /ãn/ and /n/.

(h) false liaison in /z/ occurs with *leur: on leurs a demandé.* (Alternatively, one could claim that *leur* has been re-analyzed as /lœz/.)

In the following discussion of morphophonological rules, we will make no attempt to provide a detailed formalization of the rules, but will use certain notational conventions as a shorthand. At the same time, the optional or obligatory status of the rule is difficult to determine, given the variability of the phenomena involved. The infrequent application of certain minor rules will be specified (rules are major unless otherwise indicated), as will the fact that some rules create the contexts in which others may apply (and would consequently be ordered earlier in a formal grammar). Finally, we should note that the selection of various allomorphs determined by the structure of the morphological operations of (20) precedes the morphophonological processes of (21).

(21) MORPHOPHONOLOGICAL PROCESSES

(a) *ʒ-deletion*: ʒ → ø / __ + m. The pronoun *je* deletes on occasion before *me: je m'en vais* /mãvɑ/. (minor)

(b) *Schwa deletion*: ə → ø / $\begin{cases} \_\_(\#)V \\ VC\_\_ \end{cases}$

This formulation of schwa deletion represents a gross simplification of a much more widespread and complex set of alternations. This brief statement is intended to outline only those features that are essential in the discussion of the pronouns, as in *je lé ai vu* or *jé te lé donne*.

(c) *r-deletion*: r → ø / __ # C. The final /r/ of certain prepositions (*sur, pour, par*) deletes preceding consonants. This rule then feeds (creates the environment for) both *l*-deletion and rules resolving hiatus (glide formation, fusion etc.): *sur la table* /sürlatab/ → /sülatab/ → /süatab/ → /saːtab/. (minor)

(d) *l-deletion*: l → ø / V # __ V #
$$\begin{bmatrix} \text{article} \\ \text{pronoun} \end{bmatrix}$$
(The boundaries are necessary to prevent deletion in word-internal position.) The *l* of *la* and *les* deletes in intervocalic position: *je la vois* /ʒavwɑ/, *je les vois* /ʒevwɑ/. *l*-deletion feeds glide formation, elision, fusion and nasal assimilation.

(e) *Gemination*: l, n → ll, nn / V# __ #V. When /l/ in an object pronoun (not article) does not delete, it is geminated, as is the /n/ representing *en*: *je l'ai* /ʒəlle/, *tu en as* /tünnɑ/.

(f) *Glide formation*: $\begin{bmatrix} V \\ +\text{high} \end{bmatrix}$ → G / __ (#)V
High vowels preceding vowels become glides: *tous les hommes* /twezɔm/, *on lui a parlé* /ɔ̃japarle/.

(g) *Post-vocalic glide formation*: V → G / $\begin{bmatrix} V \\ -\text{high} \end{bmatrix}$ __
On rare occasions, the VV sequences arising from *l*-deletion may become VG sequences: *à l'école* /ajkɔl/, *dans l'église* /dɑ̃jgliz/. (minor, infrequent)

(h) *Elision*: V → ø / __ # V. Certain V#V sequences produced by *l*-deletion are simplified by the deletion of the first vowel: *tu les a eus* /tezaü/, *c'est la musique* /samüzik/. (minor)

(i) *Vowel fusion*: $\begin{bmatrix} V \\ -\text{round} \end{bmatrix}$ V → V:

Two vowels often merge into a single long vowel. The quality of the resulting vowel is a combination of that of the input vowels. (Back or round initial vowels are resistant to fusion.) *il lui donne...* /iːdɔn/, *dans la maison* /dãːmezɔ̃/.

(j) *Nasal assimilation*: Ṽ # V → ṼṼ. The second vowel in a Ṽ # V sequence, or the long vowel resulting from a merger, takes on the nasality of the initial vowel: *avant les examens* /avãɛ̃zɛgzamɛ̃/, *dans la glace* /dãːglas/.

This concludes our survey of the morphophonology of CF. Before concluding in general, however, it would be appropriate to outline, in broad terms, various other morphological properties of popular French, CF in particular.

6.6 Remarks on CF morphology

We will make no attempt at completeness in this section—the morphology and syntax of popular French remain vast and seldom explored domains. We will see, however, that CF exhibits many of the same traits as popular French in general, and that it exemplifies virtually every mechanism of morphological change, where no area of the grammar remains untouched. (See, for example, Cardinal 1980, Bougaïeff 1975.) We may begin this list of illustrations with two remarks on further changes in the pronominal system. First, post-verbal stressed pronouns show special allomorphs. *le*, for example, is usually /le/ rather than /lə/, as in *si tu le veux, prends-le* /... prãle/. Whether this pronunciation is arrived at by analogy to other pronouns—*écoute-moi* /ekutmwe/ or *gêne-toi pas* /ʒɛntwepɑ/—or by other mechanisms, remains to be determined. It is also the case that the use of *ça* as a pronoun subject is expanding, accompanied on occasion by a reinforcement in /l/ of obscure origin:

(22) ça sait pas conduire   /sasepɑkɔ̃dɥir/
      ça existe pas   /saleɡzistəpɑ/
      ça oublie tout   /salublitut/
      ça a du goût   /salɑdügu/
      ça arrive   /salariv/

In the final four examples, a hypothesis linking *ça* with *cela* in liaison contexts (prevocalically) must be viewed as tempting.

The prepositional system of CF is also undergoing significant change, as demonstrated in a recent series of papers by Canale et al. (e.g. 1979, although the applicability of their results to CF in general remains to be determined). While the details of such changes would be more appropriate in a discussion of CF syntax, we may note in the prepositional domain the frequent occurrence of "compounded" forms of *de*, illustrated in (23).

(23) descends de là   /... dədlɑ/
      parle-moi de ça   /... dətsɑ/
      il vient de loin   /... dədlwɛ̃/ (less frequent)

The verb system furnishes without doubt the most extensive set of morphological innovations in CF, innovations which affect both the stem and the inflectional system. We may, in addition, find both isolated or sporadic changes, as well as more systematic modifications. Among the former are the pronunciation of *je suis* as /ʃt/ before vowels and /ʃü/ before consonants:

(24) je suis après le faire /ʃtaprɛlfajr – ʃüaprɛlfajr/
      je suis allé   /ʃtale – ʃüale/
      je suis pas allé   /ʃüpɑale/
      je suis fatigué de ça   /ʃüfatigedətsɑ/

One also finds the second singular form *es* with a final /t/: *t'est un pas bon!*, indicating a generalization of the liaison consonant throughout the singular paradigm. Such forms are frequent in popular French. Even more common, however, are examples where one verb stem, usually from a marked category, has been remodelled on the basis of a more frequent or more basic form. Subjunctives switch to indicative stems, non-third person to third person, past to present stems and so on. This is not an absolute directionality, since there are cases where singular and third plural forms are remodelled on the basis of the first and second plural forms, but in general the third singular is dominant. The extent of this process of stem restructuring in CF provides further data for the sophisticated theories of morphological structure being developed by Bybee and her co-workers (see Bybee 1980, Bybee and Brewer 1980, for example). Various types of verb stem analogies are illustrated in (25).

(25)   *SF*   *CF*   *Possible source*

SF	*CF*	*Possible source*
je vais	*je vas* /vɑ/	*va/vas*
que j'aille	*que je alle* /al/	*aller*
je suis	*je soie* /swaj – sɛj/	*soyons*
vous dîtes	*vous disez* /dize/	*disons/disent*
vous faîtes	*vous faisez* /fəze/	*faisiez/faisait*
se taire, tait etc.	*taiser* /tɛze/ *taise*, etc.	*taisons*
il nettoie plus other infinitives in -oyer)	*il nettoye* /nɛtwaj/	*nettoyons*
il bout	*il bouille* /buj/	*bouillir*
ils allaient	*ils vontaient* /võtɛ/	regularized imperfect:
ils faisaient	*ils fontaient* /fõtɛ/	third plural stem + *aient*
ils étaient	*ils sontaient* /sõtɛ/ (we never find *ontaient*, however)	

To this list, one could add a variety of regularized or remodelled infinitive or past participle forms: *tiendre, contiendre, reviendre, conviendre, taiser, poner* (*pondre*), *suir* (*suivre*); *taisé, mouru, éteindu, poursuit, sui, li* etc. Many of these reflect the influence of certain basic forms in the morphological system; others are more sporadic. There is one further, general tendency that is worthy of comment, both for its intrinsic interest and for the link it provides to innovations in liaison behaviour. Verb stems ending in vowels manifest a general tendency to insert a final consonant (at least in the present indicative and subjunctive). Monosyllabic stems such as *jouer, louer*, insert /z/, while polysyllabic forms take /s/ or /z/:

(26)   *qu'il(s) loue(nt)*   /luz/   (*louse*)
       qu'il joue   /ʒuz/   (*jouse*)
       qu'ils se marient   /maris/ or   (*marissent/marisent*)
                          /mariz/
       ils s'assoient   /sasiz/   (*s'assisent*)
       il conclut   /kɔ̃klüz/   (*concluse*)
       ils étudient   /etüdis/   (*étudissent*)

The models for these innovations are to be found in the "-ir" conjugation for the insertion of /s/: *il finit – ils finissent*, and in frequent verbs *lire, dire, luire, élire* for /z/-insertion (reinforced, no doubt, by the role of /z/ as a plural liaison consonant) in the case of the monosyllables. The phenomenon of liaison is a complex one in French (see Tranel 1981 for a recent survey); in particular, popular or colloquial French shows many cases of "false" liaison, where a consonant (usually /z/, /t/ or /n/) is inserted between vowels within a phonological phrase, even when this consonant is not expected in SF. In many cases, the consonant /z/ (the most frequent) can be linked to a semantically plural context, /n/ to a nasal environment, and /t/ to a third person verb form as model. Finally, certain occurrences of hiatus are simply broken up by an inserted consonant for phonotactic reasons. Representative CF examples of this very widespread phenomenon are to be seen in (27).

(27)　FALSE LIAISON

on y va	/ɔ̃ziva/
la Faculté y va	/lafakülteziva/
quatre hommes	/katzɔm/
huit enfants	/ɥizɑ̃fɑ̃/
donne-moi-en	/dɔnmwazɑ̃/
on leur a dit	/ɔ̃lœrzadi/
donne-lui	/dɔnzi/
sous une forme ou une autre	/suzünfɔrmuzünotr/
il en a	/inɑ̃na/
tu en veux d'autres	/tünɑ̃vødot/
t'es un pas bon	/tetœ̃pabɔ̃/ (analogy with *est*)
je suis allé	/stale/
il y en a une	/jɑ̃natün/
il s'en va avec Marcel	/isɑ̃nvatavɛk.../

Let us close this section with a brief survey of a second phenomenon involving final consonants. It is clear that in SF, the presence versus the absence of a final consonant indicates feminine versus masculine gender: *grand – grande* /grɑ̃/ – /grɑ̃d/, *petit – petite* /pəti/ – /pətit/, etc. This distinction has been extended in popular French, including CF which has pairs such as the following:

(28)
　　　　　　avare – avar*de*
　　　　　　cru – cru*te*
　　　　　　favori – favori*te*
　　　　　　pourri – pourri*te*
　　　　　　pointu – pointu*s*e
　　　　　　bossu – bossu*s*e

Both the liaison and the adjectival examples serve again to emphasize the important morphological role played by final consonants in French.

It is time to close this brief survey. We have not been able to consider a host of further attributes of CF features that would lead us far afield. No discussion of the CF lexicon, so rich both in loans and neologisms, is possible. Nor can we delve into the various syntactic innovations that also characterize Canada's official Romance language. Yet in spite of its specific attributes, CF is still clearly a close relative of SF. The great majority of traits, both phonological and morphological, that occur in the popular language of Canada can also be discovered in continental varieties. As has so often been noted, we must not confuse geography with the notion of level or style. Nevertheless, if the individual properties of CF, taken in isolation, remain rooted in corresponding traits from other dialects or styles, it is nonetheless clear that the combination of this series of innovations into a distinctly Canadian pattern results in a variety of French that is full of vitality and viability for its speakers, and of interest for the scientific community involved in dialectal and sociolinguistic studies. I hope this small volume has served to emphasize these attributes.

FURTHER READING—CF MORPHOPHONOLOGY

Morphophonology is a complex domain, encompassing many aspects of both phonology and morphology. A general explanation of the concept may be found in Fischer-Jørgensen 1975, while Schane 1968, Dell 1980 and Tranel 1981a all treat aspects of SF morphophonology. Rigault 1971 also contains much relevant information. As for CF, Morin 1979 and Prairie 1976 are not limited to single topics, while the works to follow are more specific in nature.

Deletion of /l/: Bougaïeff and Cardinal (1980)
                Laliberté (1974)
                Poplack and Walker (1983)
                Pupier and Légaré (1973)
                Pupier and Pelchat (1972)
                Sankoff and Cedergren (1971a, b)
                Santerre, Noiseux and Ostiguy (1977)
Vowel fusion: Dumas (1974a)
                Santerre and Ostiguy (1978)
                Villa (1977)
Liaison, analogy, morphology in general:
                Morin (1981)
                Picard (1981)
                Van Ameringen and Cedergren (1981)

Finally, much information in the latter areas, as well as an appreciation for the structure of the CF lexicon in general, may be obtained from Dulong and Bergeron 1980 as well as from the following dictionaries of CF. (The first two have been subject to a considerable amount of criticism.)

                Belisle, L.-A. (1957)
                Bergeron, L. (1980)
                Clapin (1974)
                Dunn (1976)
                Société du Parler français au Canada (1930)

Appendix 1

Phonological Features

In Appendix 1, we tabulate the set of binary phonological features used in this work, giving one or more defining properties and illustrating the classes of sounds established by each feature. A "+" value indicates the presence of the property denoted by the feature, while a "−" indicates its absence. More detailed discussion of distinctive feature theory and of different feature inventories may be found in Chomsky and Halle 1968, Dell 1980, Fischer-Jørgensen 1975, Schane 1973 or Sommerstein 1977, among many other references. Commonly used abbreviations for the feature names are given in parentheses.

1. [sonorant] ([son]) refers to highly resonant sounds produced with a free flow of air through the oral or nasal cavities and with large amounts of acoustic energy. Vowels, nasals, liquids and glides are [+sonorant]. [−sonorant] sounds, the *obstruents*, including stops, fricatives and affricates, are produced with a significant restriction of the air flow, a restriction which may include complete blockage, as in the stops and affricates.
2. [syllabic] ([syl]) sounds are able to constitute the nucleus of syllables. Vowels and, much less frequently, other sonorant segments are [+syllabic].
3. [consonantal] ([cons]) refers to sounds produced with considerable narrowing of the air passage in the oral cavity. Obstruents, liquids and nasals are [+consonantal].
4. [continuant] ([cont]) refers to sounds whose articulation can be prolonged. Fricatives, nasals, liquids, glides and vowels are [+continuant].
5. [nasal] ([nas]) refers to sounds produced with a lowered velum and consequently with air flow through the nasal passages. Nasal consonants ([m n ɲ ŋ] etc.) and nasalized vowels are [+nasal].
6. [high] groups together the high and higher-mid vowels [i, e, u, o] as opposed to the lower-mid and low vowels ([ɛ æ a ɑ ɔ]).
7. [mid] groups together the higher-mid and lower-mid vowels

([e ε o ɔ]) and opposes them to both the high vowels and the low vowels.

8. [back] refers to the distinction between front versus back vowels. (Special measures must be taken to identify central vowels, which are neither front nor back.)

9. [round] ([rnd]) refers to sounds produced with rounded lips, such as [ü u o ɔ]. (Consonants may also be rounded, as is the *t* in *twin*, for example.)

10. [tense] ([tns]) is a controversial feature, since its articulatory correlates are not firmly established. It usually refers to vowels produced with greater muscular tension, greater duration and greater deviation from the mid-point of the articulatory space. Thus [i ü u] are [+tense], while [I Ü U] are [–tense], i.e. lax. The use of [±tense] to distinguish higher-mid from lower-mid vowels remains the subject of debate, as does its use to differentiate voiceless ([+tense]) from voiced ([–tense]) obstruents.

11. [anterior] ([ant]) refers to consonants whose point of constriction occurs in the forward part of the oral cavity. Labials, dentals and alveolars are [+anterior]; alveopalatals, palatals and velars are [–anterior].

12. [coronal] ([cor]) sounds have the blade of the tongue as primary articulator. Dentals, alveolars and palatals are [+coronal]; labials and velars are [–coronal].

13. [voice] ([vce]) refers to sounds produced with accompanying vibration of the vocal cords. Vowels, nasals, liquids and glides are normally voiced. Obstruents may be voiced or voiceless.

14. [delayed release] ([del rel]) is relevant only to distinguish affricates from the corresponding stops. [t d] are [–delayed release]; [t^s d^z č ǰ] are [+delayed release].

15. [strident] ([str]) sounds have greater acoustic noisiness than their non-strident counterparts. Affricates are [+strident] compared to the corresponding stops, while among fricatives, [s z ʃ ʒ] are [+strident] compared to [θ ð].

16. [lateral] ([lat]) sounds are produced with the middle part of the oral cavity blocked, and with the airstream passing over the sides of the tongue. [l ɬ λ] are [+lateral] liquids; [r̃ ř R] are [–lateral] liquids.

Appendix 2

Glossary

This glossary defines briefly some of the more technical terms to be found in the preceding analysis. Fuller treatment may be found in one of several dictionaries of linguistics, such as Pei 1966 or Dubois et al. 1973, in any of the standard general manuals (Bloomfield 1933, Hockett 1965, Lyons 1968, among many others) or in the phonological texts noted in Appendix 1.

allomorph: a variant of a morpheme that occurs in a specific context. Allomorphs may be conditioned by phonological context, e.g. the English plural *s* is pronounced /əz/ after coronal fricatives and affricates (*buses, churches, judges*, etc.); /s/ after other voiceless segments, (*mops, hats*, etc.), and /z/ after other voiced segments, including vowels (*buns, ribs, seas*, etc.). In other cases, allomorphs are conditioned by their grammatical or lexical environments. Thus, certain English plural noun stems end in a voiced fricative, while their singular counterpart ends in a voiceless fricative: *knife – knives, house – houses*, etc. The area of linguistics dealing with the phonological changes within allomorphs of one and the same morpheme is known as morphophonemics or morphophonology.

allophone: a positional variant of a phoneme. In English, stops are aspirated at the beginning of words [p^h t^h k^h] (*pin, tin, kin*) but unaspirated [p t k] after [s] (*spin, stun, skin*). In CF, high vowels are tense in word-final position, but lax before voiceless consonants: [i ü u] in *vie, vue, vous* versus [I Ü U] in *fils, jupe, coupe* and so on. Allophones may be completely determined by context, as in the preceding examples, or in free variation, i.e. alternating in form without any difference of meaning, as in English stops in final position, which may be indifferently aspirated or unaspirated: [hɔt^h] or [hɔt] for *hot*.

analogy: in the most general terms, the transfer of a linguistic feature from one form to another; the extension of a pattern to forms not showing the feature; the regularization of irregular forms. Examples of analogy: *one foot – two foots, nous faisons – vous faisez*, CF *ils jousent, lousent* for *jouent, louent*.

aspirate-h: in French phonology, the name given to a sub-class of words which behave as if their pronunciation began with a consonant, even though they are vowel-initial. Consequently, "h-aspiré" words do not show elision or liaison: *le héro* [ləero] – *les héros* [leero].

assibilation: a type of assimilation whereby apical stop consonants become affricates by developing a sibilant ('s-type') release. [t^s d^z] are assibilants, developed from [t d].

assimilation: a process whereby two sounds acquire common characteristics through the transference of properties from one to the other. Palatalization, nasalization, vowel harmony are all assimilatory processes.

clitic (proclitic, enclitic): an unaccented word or morpheme which is phonologically dependent on surrounding words. Proclitics precede the host; enclitics follow it. In French, the subject and object pronouns are proclitics. In Latin *que* 'and' is an enclitic, attached to the preceding word.

continuant: a consonant that may be continued or prolonged without alteration of its articulation. Continuants include fricatives, laterals and (usually) nasals, but exclude stops and affricates.

diphthong: the combination of a vowel and a semi-vowel into a single syllable; a long vowel of changing aperture. In English, we see clear diphtongs in *buy, bough, boy*; in French, the digraph *oi* has various diphthongal realizations.

elision: the deletion of a vowel. In French, more specifically, the simplification of *le, la* and sometimes *si* before vowels: *l'arc, l'écume, s'il vient*.

epenthesis: the insertion of a transitional segment between two sounds or at the limits of words: Latin *camera* > French *chambre*; *scola* > Spanish *escuela*; English *"athelete"* < athlete, *"filum"* < *film*, etc.

free variation: the occurrence of different sounds optionally in the same environment without producing any change of meaning: English aspirated versus non-aspirated stops in final position ([hɔtʰ – hɔt]); French [o – ɔ] in pretonic open syllables ([poto – pɔto] 'poteau').

geminate: doubling or prolonging of a consonant, either morpheme-internally (Italian *fatto*) or between morphemes (French *netteté, il l'a*; English *book-case*), etc.

glide: (see *semi-vowel*)

joual: a spoken variety of Quebec French, often stigmatized, identified with the lower-class speech of urban areas (especially Montreal) and characterized by a great extent of phonetic reduction.

laxing: the process by which tense vowels become lax, usually in closed syllables. Thus *vie* [vi] versus *ville* [vIl], etc. in CF.

liaison: (false liaison): the pronunciation of an otherwise silent (latent) final consonant when the following word begins with a vowel: French *petit garçon* vs *petit ami*. False liaison involves the insertion of an "incorrect" or non-etymological liaison consonant: *quatre-z hommes, on-z y va*.

loi-de-position: the tendency in French for the higher-mid (closed) vowels to occur in open syllables and the lower-mid (open) vowels to occur in closed syllables: *sot* [so] versus *sotte* [sɔt]; *peu* [pø] versus *peur* [pœr], etc.

mellowing: in CF, the pronunciation of the palatal fricatives [ʃ ʒ] as less strident, weakened, velar or pharyngeal fricatives. Often identified with the Beauce region, although actually more widespread.

metathesis: transposition in the order of sounds: Latin *miraculum* > Spanish *milagro*, CF *berbis* < *brebis*, *ervient* < *revient*, etc.

morpheme (morphology): minimal meaningful unit used in the construction of words; classified as roots and affixes. *informal* consists of three morphemes: a prefix *in-*, a root *form* and a suffix *-al*. *cats* consists of two morphemes: the root *cat* and the plural suffix *-s*. Morphology is the study of the structure and arrangement of morphemes or, in more general terms, of the structure of words.

morphophonology (morphophonemics): the study of the different forms of the allomorphs of a single morpheme. The different allomorphs of the prefix *in-*, /Im- In- Iŋ -/ (*impossible, intolerable, incongruous*) present a morphophonemic alternation, as do the masculine-feminine French adjective pairs *petit – petite, grand – grande, heureux – heureuse, gentil – gentille, bon – bonne*, etc., where a final consonant is present in the feminine but absent in the masculine.

neutralization: the temporary suspension, in a specific phonological context, of a phonemic difference that is normally functional. In English, /i/ and /I/ are different phonemes (*beat-bit*), but the difference is neutralized before /r/, where only one of the two can occur, or in word-final position, where only /i/ is found. In French, the /o/ – /ɔ/ opposition (*saute, sotte*) is neutralized in final position, from where /ɔ/ is excluded.

obstruent: a consonant produced with significant obstruction in the oral cavity and with little acoustic energy, compared to sonorants. Stops, fricatives and affricates are obstruents; vowels, glides, nasals and liquids are sonorants. (see *sonorant*)

paradigm: in phonology, the complete inventory of the phonemes of a language, arranged in the pattern determined by their place and manner of articulation. In morphology, a paradigm consists of the complete set of conjugational, declensional or derived forms of a word, as in *run, runs, ran, running, runner, run* (noun).

phonotactics: the study of sequences of phonemes, the position in which phonemes can occur, the constraints on combinations of phonemes.

pretonic: occurring in a syllable preceding the stressed (or tonic) syllable. In the French word *demain, -main* is the stressed syllable, *de-* is the pretonic syllable.

productive: the relative frequency with which new forms may be introduced into a language; the normal or regular pattern which tends to be extended to irregular forms. In English, the productive plural pattern is to use the suffix *-s*, so irregular forms (*foot, deer, octopus*) tend to assimilate to this productive pattern.

prosody: the quantitative, accentual or melodic aspects of sounds; the study of length, stress, tone and intonation involves prosody.

Prosodic elements are inherently relative, analyzed by comparison to equivalent features in adjacent syllables.

rule: an explicit, often formalized description of the regularities in a body of data, or of the correspondences between (sets of) linguistic forms. Linguists have developed a wide variety of rules, including allophonic rules, which account for different realizations (allophones) of phonemes depending on context; and morphophonemic rules, which describe the phonological differences between allomorphs of the same morpheme. Rules may have different properties: they may be *obligatory*, always applying, or *optional*, accounting for free variation. Optional rules are often *variable*, applying with greater or lesser frequency depending on stylistic or social factors. Finally, *minor* rules account for regularities in subsets of data that are not typical of the language as a whole, while *major* rules are productive, typical of the whole lexicon and normally obligatory. In any event, rules in current linguistics are descriptive devices, not the normative or prescriptive statements of traditional teaching.

Examples of rule types:

allophonic: aspirated stops word-initially in English; non-aspirated after *s*.

morphophonemic: the allomorphs /Im/, /In/, /Iŋ/ of the English prefix *in-*.

obligatory: both of the above rules are obligatory.

optional: the rule deleting word-final /t/ before words beginning with a consonant: *he kept coming, he slept late*. This rule is also *variable*, depending on style, grammatical category, rate of speech and so on.

major: the first two rules exemplified are major rules. (The morphophonemic rule also applies in other cases of nasal assimilation.)

minor: the rule describing the voicing differences of the final fricatives in some plural forms in English is a minor rule (*knife – knives, leaf – leaves*, etc.).

schwa (*e*-caduc, *e*-muet): an unaccented, indistinct, neutral vowel, represented by orthographic *e* in French, that is subject to deletion on a variety of phonological, grammatical or stylistic grounds. It is deleted in such words as *nous v∅nons, sam∅di, petit∅, pas l∅ mien*, etc.

semi-vowel (glide): a non-syllabic segment corresponding in position of articulation to a high vowel, and combining with vowels to form complex syllabic nuclei or diphthongs. In English [j] and [w] are semi-vowels; in French, [j], [ɥ] and [w].

sonorant: a sound produced with unrestricted air flow and high (and periodic) acoustic energy. Vowels, liquids, nasals and glides are sonorants. (See *obstruent*, as well as Appendix 1).

stress: relative prominence given to a syllable, in contrast to its neighbours, through increased loudness, duration or pitch (or a combination of these). In French the last syllable of the word is stressed (or accented).

suppletion (suppletive): the situation obtaining when the allomorphs of a morpheme bear little or no phonological resemblance to one another. In English, *go* and *went*; *am, is, are, was, were* are suppletive allomorphs of the verb stems for *to go* and *to be* respectively. In French, the verb *aller* has suppletive allomorphs of the stem: *vais, allons, irons*.

syllable (open and closed syllable): precise articulatory or acoustic definitions of the syllable are problematic; it is often identified with a chest pulse in respiratory terms or with a peak of sonority. More simply, it may be defined as a vowel accompanied by all non-syllabic material (consonants, glides) associated with it. Thus, *oh* [o], *I* [aj], *in* [In], *breadth* [brɛdθ] constitute single syllables, while *compost* [kɔm-post] is composed of two syllables, and so on. Open syllables end in vowels (*bee* [bi]); closed syllables end in consonants (*in* [In]).

velarization: a process whereby sounds become pronounced in the velar region or with velar co-articulation. The passage of [ɲ] to [ŋ] is a case of velarization in CF; the 'dark' allophone of /l/ in English in *milk* or *pill* is a velarized allophone, combining [l] and [w] qualities.

vowel harmony: an assimilatory process whereby vowels, usually in adjacent syllables, must agree in some property (backness, rounding, tenseness). When, in CF, the vowel in the first syllable of *minute* is laxed, it is by harmony to the lax vowel of the final syllable: [mInÜt].

Appendix 3

List of Rules

We give here the list of rules dealing with the CF phenomena of Chapers 3-6, followed by a reference to the section where the relevant material is discussed and exemplified.

Process	*Section*
Vowel length – intrinsically long vowels	3.1
– lengthening consonants	3.1
– pretonic lengthening	3.1
Vowel laxing – stressed vowels	3.2
– high vowels	3.2.1
Laxing harmony	3.2.2
Initial syllable laxing	3.2.2
Diphthongization	3.3
Devoicing	3.4
Vowel deletion	3.5
Backing	3.6
Lowering of /ɛ/	3.7
Diphthong *oi* – *w*-deletion	3.8
Metathesis	3.10
Lowering of /ɛ/ preceding /r/	3.11
Assibilation	4.1
Final consonant deletion	4.2
Nasal assimilation	4.4
Velarization of /ɲ/	4.5
/l/ deletion	6.2, 6.3
Gemination	6.4
Glide formation	6.4
Elision	6.4
Fusion	6.4

BIBLIOGRAPHY

Anttila, R. 1972. An Introduction to Historical and Comparative Linguistics. New York: Macmillan.

Baligand, R. 1973. The intonation of wh-questions in Franco-ontarian. Canadian Journal of Linguistics 18.2, 89–101.

Baligand, R. and E. James. 1973. Les structures mélodiques de la phrase interrogative lexicale en franco-ontarien. In Grundstrom and Léon 1973, 123–167.

Baligand, R. and E. James. 1979. Contribution à l'étude de la durée vocalique en franco-canadien. In Léon and Rossi 1979, 55–64.

Bauche, H. 1920. Le langage populaire. Paris: Payot.

Beauchemin, N. 1972. Quelques traits de prononciation québécoise dans un contexte anglophone qui les influence. Recherches socio-linguistiques dans la région de Sherbrooke, document n° 2. Université de Sherbrooke.

Beauchemin, N. 1977. La diphtongaison en estrie, socio- ou géo-linguistique? In Walter 1977, 9–24.

Bélisle, L.-A. 1957. Dictionnaire général de la langue française au Canada. Québec: Bélisle.

Bergeron, L. 1980. Dictionnaire de la langue québécoise. Montréal: VLB Éditeur.

Bloomfield, L. 1933. Language. New York: Holt, Rinehart and Winston.

Bossé, D. and A. Dugas. 1983. La fin de l'histoire d'un des deux A. Paper presented at the 1983 Canadian Linguistic Association meetings, Vancouver, B.C.

Boudreault, M. 1968. Rythme et mélodie de la phrase parlée en France et au Québec. Paris: Klincksieck.

Boudreault, M. 1970. Le rythme en langue franco-canadienne. In Léon, Faure and Rigault 1970, 21-32.

Bougaïeff, A. 1975. Étude de morphologie et de phonétique: l'article défini et le pronom personnel de troisième personne dans le parler populaire du Québec. Thèse de doctorat. Université Laval.

Bougaïeff, A. and P. Cardinal. 1980. La chute du /l/ dans le parler populaire du Québec. La linguistique 16.2, 91–102.
Bouthillier, G. and J. Maynard (eds.). 1972. Le choc des langues au Québec 1760–1970. Montréal: Presses de l'Université du Québec.
Brent, E. 1970. Canadian French: A Synthesis. Ph.D. Dissertation. Cornell University.
Brunelle, A. and C. Tousignant. 1981. L'autocorrection chez un sujet Montréalais: étude quantitative. In Sankoff and Cedergren (eds.) 1981, 25–31.
Bybee, J. 1980. Child morphology and morphophonemic change. In Historical Morphology. J. Fisiak (ed.) The Hague: Mouton, 157–187.
Bybee, J. and M. Brewer. 1980. Explanation in morphophonemics: Changes in Provençal and Spanish preterite forms. Lingua 52, 271–312.
Bynon, T. 1977. Historical Linguistics. Cambridge: CUP.
Canale, M., R. Mougeon, M. Bélanger and C. Main. 1977. Recherches en dialectologie franco-ontarienne. Working Papers on Bilingualism 14, 1–20.
Canale, M., R. Mougeon and M. Bélanger. 1978. Analogical levelling of the auxiliary *être* in Ontarian French. In Contemporary Studies in Romance Linguistics. M. Suner (ed.). Washington: Georgetown University Press.
Canale, M., R. Mougeon and E. Beniak. 1979. Generalization of *pour* after verbs of motion in Ontarian French. In the Fifth Lacus Forum. A. Makkai (ed.). Columbia: Hornbeam Press.
Cardinal, P. 1980. L'énoncé franco-québécois populaire. Étude syntaxique. Thèse de doctorat. Université de Paris – Sorbonne.
Cedergren, H. 1983. La variation métrique et la réduction de voyelles dans le français de Montréal. Paper presented at the 1983 NWAVE conference, Montreal, P.Q.
Cedergren, H.J., J. Clermont and F. Coté. 1981. Le facteur temps et deux diphtongues du français montréalais. In Sankoff and Cedergren (eds.) 1981, 169–176.

Chambers, J. 1975. Canadian English. Origins and Structures. Toronto: Methuen.
Chambers, J. and P. Trudgill. 1980. Dialectology. Cambridge: CUP.
Charbonneau, R. 1955. Recherche d'une norme phonétique dans la région de Montréal. Études sur le parler français au Canada. Société du parler français au Canada. Québec: Presses de l'Université Laval, 83-98.
Charbonneau, R. 1957. La spirantisation du /ž/. Canadian Journal of Linguistics 3, 14-19, 71-77.
Charbonneau, R. 1971. Les voyelles nasales du franco-canadien (région de Montréal): étude de phonétique expérimentale. Paris: Klincksieck.
Charbonneau, R. and B. Jacques, 1972. [t^s] et [d^z] en français canadien. In Valdman (ed.) 1972, 77-90.
Charbonneau, R. and A. Marchal. 1976. Considérations sur la définition acoustique et perceptuelle des "R" en français québecois. In Rondeau et al. 1976, 291-303.
Chomsky, N. and M. Halle. 1968. The Sound Pattern of English. New York: Harper and Row.
Clapin, S. 1974. Dictionnaire canadien-français. (Reproduction de l'édition originale de 1894). Québec: Presses de l'Université Laval.
Clayton 1981. Word boundaries and sandhi rules in natural generative phonology. Language 57.3, 571-590.
Clermont, J. and H. Cedergren. 1979. Les 'R' de ma mère sont perdus dans l'air. In Thibault (ed.) 1979, 13-28.
Connors, K., K. Lappin and P. Pupier. 1981. Les petits enfants bilingues sont-ils si différents des unilingues? Quelques observations sur la phonologie d'enfants bilingues. In Sankoff and Cedergren (eds.) 1981, 153-159.
Corbeil, J.-C. and L. Guilbert (eds.) 1976. Le français au Québec. Langue française 31.
Corbett, N. 1975. Review of Le rythme et la mélodie de la phrase littéraire dans l'oeuvre de Mgr. F.-A. Savard: Essai de phonostylistique, by Gilles Lavoie; Étude sur les voyelles nasales du français canadien, by René Charbonneau; Recherches sur la structure phonique du français canadien,

by Pierre Léon. Romance Philology XXVIII, 3, 1975, 379–383.
Corne, J.C. 1965. Enquête sur le français régional au Canada. Te Reo 8, 62–66.
Darnell, R. (ed.), 1971. Linguistic Diversity in Canadian Society. Edmonton: Linguistic Research Inc.
de Saussure, F. 1916. Cours de linguistique générale. Paris: Payot.
Dehaies, D. 1981. Le français parlé dans la ville de Québec. Une étude sociolinguistique. Québec: Centre international de recherche sur le bilinguisme.
Deshaies-Lafontaine, D. 1974. A Socio-phonetic Study of a Quebec French Community: Trois-Rivières. Ph.D. Thesis, U. of London.
Delattre, P. 1968. Review of Gendron 1966. Language 44, 852–855.
Delattre, P. 1971. Review of Bouldreault 1968. Romance Philology 25, 121–123.
Dell, F. 1973a. Les règles et les sons. Paris: Hermann.
Dell, F. 1973b. 'e muet', fiction graphique ou réalité linguistique? In Anderson, S. and P. Kiparsky (eds.). A Festschrift for Morris Halle. New York: Holt, Rinehart and Winston, 26–50.
Dell, F. 1980. Generative Phonology and French Phonology (Translation by C. Cullen of Dell 1973a). Cambridge: CUP.
Démarchais, G. 1976. De la phonétique à la phonologie d'un idiolecte québécois. In Rondeau, G., G. Bibeau, G. Gagné and G. Taggart (eds.) 1976, Montréal: CEC, 261–290.
Diller, Anne-Marie. 1978. The mute E in French as a sociolinguistic variable. Montreal Working Papers in Linguistics *10* (ed. by Y.-C. Morin and A. Querido).
Dubois, J., M. Giacomo, L. Guespin, C. Marcellesi, J.-B. Marcellesi and J.-P. Mevel. 1973. Dictionnaire de linguistique. Paris: Larousse.
Dulong, G. 1966. Bibliographie linguistique du Canada français. Paris: Klincksieck.
Dulong, G. and G. Bergeron. 1980. Le parler populaire du Québec et de ses régions limitrophes. Atlas linguistique de l'est du Canada. Québec: Éditeur officiel du Québec.

Dumas, D. 1974a. La fusion vocalique en français québécois. Recherches linguistiques à Montréal 2, 23-51.
Dumas, D. 1974b. Durée vocalique et diphtongaison en français québécois. Cahier de linguistique 4,13-55.
Dumas, D. 1976. Quebec French high vowel harmony: the progression of a phonological rule. Chicago Linguistic Society 12, 161-168.
Dumas, D. 1978. Phonologie des réductions vocaliques en français québécois. Thèse de Ph.D. Université de Montréal.
Dumas, D. 1981. Structure de la diphtongaison québécoise. Canadian Journal of Linguistics 26.1, 1-61.
Dumas, D. and A. Boulanger. 1981. Les matériaux d'origine des voyelles fermées du français québécois. Revue Québécoise de Linguistique 11.2, 49-72.
Dunn, O. 1976. Glossaire franco-canadien (Reproduction de l'édition originale de 1880). Québec: Presses de l'Université Laval.
Encrevé, P. 1983. La liaison sans enchaînement. Actes de la recherche en sciences sociales, 46, 39-66.
Fischer-Jørgensen, E. 1975. Trends in Phonological Theory. Copenhagen: Akademisk Forlag.
Foley, J. 1977. Foundations of Theoretical Phonology. Cambridge: CUP.
Fonagy, I. 1979. L'accent français: accent probabilitaire. In Léon and Fonagy (eds.) 1979: 123-233.
Fouché, P. 1959. Traité de prononciation française. 2e édition. Paris: Klincksieck.
Frei, H. 1929. La grammaire des fautes. Paris: Geuthner.
Fromkin, V. 1978. Tone: A Linguistic Survey. New York: Academic Press.
Fromkin, V. and R. Rodman. 1983. An Introduction to Language. 3rd edition. New York: Holt.
Gendron, J.-D. 1959. Désonorisation des voyelles en franco-canadien. Canadian Journal of Linguistics 5.2, 99-108.
Gendron, J.-D. 1966a. Tendances phonétiques du français parlé au Canada. Paris: Klincksieck.

Gendron, J.-D. 1966b. Contribution à l'étude du français rural parlé au Canada. Travaux de Linguistique et de Littérature 4.1, 173-189.
Gendron, J.-D. 1967. Le phonétisme du français canadien du Québec face à l'adstrat anglo-américain. In Gendron and Straka 1967, 15-67.
Gendron, J.-D. 1970. Origine de quelques traits de prononciation du parler populaire franco-québécois. In Phonétique et linguistique romanes: mélanges offerts à M. Georges Straka, 339-352. Paris: CNRS.
Gendron, J.-D. and G. Straka (eds.). 1967. Études de linguistique canadienne. Paris: Klincksieck.
Geoffrion, L.-P. 1934. La diphtongue *oi* dans le franco-canadien. Le Canada français XXII, 4, 384-390.
Grundstrom, A. and P. Léon (eds.). 1973. Interrogation et intonation. Montréal: Didier.
Guiraud, P. 1965. Le français populaire. Paris: PUF.
Haden, E. 1941. The assibilated dentals in Franco-Canadian. American Speech 16, 285-288.
Haden, E. 1973. French dialect geography in North America. Current Trends in Linguistics 10. Linguistics in North America. T. Sebeok (ed.) The Hague: Mouton, 422-439.
Hockett, C. 1965. A Course in Modern Linguistics. New York: Macmillan.
Holder, M. 1972. Le parler populaire franco-canadien (la prononciation de quelques Canadiens français de la région de Sudbury-North-Bay). Phonetica 26, 33-49.
Hooper, J. 1976. An introduction to Natural Generative Phonology. New York: Academic Press.
Hull, A. 1956. The Franco-Canadian dialect of Windsor, Ontario: A preliminary study. Orbis 5, 35-60.
Hull, A. 1960. The shift from (sh) to (h) in Canadian French. Proceedings of the Linguistic Circle of Manitoba and North Dakota 2.2, 20-24.
Hull, A. 1966. The Structure of the Canadian French consonant system. La Linguistique 1, 103-110.
Hull, A. 1968. The Origins of New-World French phonology. Word 24, 255-269.

Hyman, L. 1975. Phonology: Theory and Analysis. New York: Holt, Rinehart and Winston.
Jackson, M. 1974. Aperçu de tendances phonétiques du parler français en Saskatchewan. Canadian Journal of Linguistics 19.2, 121–133.
Jacques, B. 1974. Variations de durée des voyelles et des consonnes fricatives postvocaliques finales de syllabe en position accentuée et unaccentuée. Cahier de linguistique 4, 89–115.
Juilland, A. 1965. Dictionnaire inverse de la langue française. The Hague: Mouton.
Juneau, M. 1972. Contribution à l'histoire de la prononciation française au Québec. Paris: Klincksieck.
Juneau, M. and G. Straka (eds.). 1975. Travaux de linguistique québécoise. Québec: Presses de l'Université Laval.
Kemp, W. 1981. Major sociolinguistic patterns in French. In Sankoff and Cedergren (eds.) 1981.
Kemp, W., P. Pupier and M. Yaeger. 1980. A linguistic and social description of final consonant cluster simplification in Montreal French. In Shuy, R. and A. Shnukal (eds.), Language Use and the Uses of Language. Washington: Georgetown University Press, 12–40.
Kemp, W. and M. Yaeger-Dror. 1981. Between [asjɔ̃] and [ɔːsjɔ̃]: changes in the realization of -ation in Quebec French. Paper presented at the 10th NWAVE Conference, Philadelphia.
Kiparsky, P. 1979. Metrical structure assignment is cyclic. Linguistic Inquiry 10, 421–442.
Laberge, S. and M. Chiasson-Lavoie. 1971. Attitudes face au français parlé à Montréal et degrés de conscience de variables linguistiques. In Darnell (ed.) 1971, 89–126.
Labov, W. 1972. Sociolinguistic Patterns. Philadephia: University of Pennsylvania Press.
Labov, W., M. Yaeger and R. Steiner. 1972. A Quantitative Study of Sound Change in Progress. Philadelphia: U.S. Regional Survey.
LaFollette, J. 1952. Étude linguistique de quatre contes folkloriques du Canada français. Thèse de doctorat. Université Laval.

LaFollette, J. 1960. Quelques observations sur le comportement du schwa en franco-canadien. Canadian Journal of Linguistics 6.1, 29–34.
Laliberté, T. 1974. L'élision du 'l' en français québécois. Lingua 33, 115–122.
Lappin, K. 1981. Évaluation de la prononciation du français montréalais: étude sociolinguistique. Revue Québécoise de Linguistique, 11.2, 93–112.
Lavoie, T. (ed.). 1979. Les français régionaux du Québec. Protée VII.2.
Lefebvre, C., L. Drapeau and C. Dubuisson (eds.). 1980. Le français parlé en milieu populaire. Recherches linguistiques à Montréal 15.
Légaré, L. 1978. Relâchement des voyelles hautes et reformulation. Cahier de linguistique 7, 31–42.
Lehiste, I. 1970. Suprasegmentals. Cambridge, Mass.: MIT Press.
Lennig, M. 1978. Acoustic Measurement of Linguistic Change: The Modern Paris Vowel System. Ph.D. Dissertation. University of Pennsylvania.
Léon, P. 1964. Prononciation du français standard. Paris: Didier.
Léon, P. 1967. /h/ et /r/ en patois normand et en français canadien. In Gendron and Straka 1967, 125–142.
Léon, P. (ed.). 1968. Recherches sur la structure phonique du français canadien. Montréal: Didier.
Léon, P. 1983. Dynamique des changements phonétiques dans le français de France et du Canada. La Linguistique 19.1.
Léon, P. and M. Nemni. 1967. Franco-canadien et français standard: problèmes de perception des oppositions vocaliques. Canadian Journal of Linguistics 12.2, 97–112.
Léon, P., G. Faure and A. Rigault (eds.). 1970. Prosodic Feature Analysis. Montréal: Didier.
Léon, P. and I. Fonagy (eds.). 1979. L'accent en français contemporain. Montréal: Didier.
Léon, P. and M. Rossi. 1979. Problèmes de prosodie. Vol. II: Expérimentations, modèles et fonctions. Montréal: Didier.
Lerond, A. 1980. Dictionnaire de la prononciation. Paris: Larousse.
Lorent, M. 1977. Le parler populaire de la Beauce. Outremont: Leméac.

Lyons, J. 1968. Introduction to Theoretical Linguistics. Cambridge: CUP.
Malmberg, B. 1969. Phonétique française. Malmö: Hermods.
Marchal, A. 1980. L'affrication de [t] et [d] en français de Montréal. Travaux de l'Institut de Phonétique d'Aix 7, 79–99.
Martinet, A. 1945. La prononciation du français contemporain. Paris: Droz.
Martinet, A. 1955. Économie des changements phonétiques. Berne: Franke.
Martinet, A. 1964. Elements of General Linguistics. London: Faber and Faber.
Martinet, A. 1969. Le français sans fard. Paris: PUF.
Martinet, A. and H. Walter. 1973. Dictionnaire de la prononciation française dans son usage réel. Paris: France-Expansion.
Massignon, G. 1962. Les parlers français d'Acadie. Enquête linguistique. Paris: Klincksieck.
Maury, N. and P. Wrenn. 1973. L'interrogation mélodique en français canadien de l'Ontario. In Grundstrom and Léon (eds.) 1973, 99–122.
Michel, A. 1882. L'accent français au Canada. Nouvelles soirées canadiennes I, 386–391.
Mettas, O. 1970. Étude sur le A dans deux sociolectes parisiens. Revue Romaine V. 1, 94–105.
Mettas, O. 1979. Quantité et rythme dans le français parlé à Paris. In Léon and Rossi (eds.) 1979, 65–78.
Morgan, R. 1975. The Regional French of County Beauce, Quebec. The Hague: Mouton.
Morin, Y.-C. 1974. Règles phonologiques à domaine indéterminé: chute du cheval en français. Cahier de linguistique 4, 69–88.
Morin. Y.-C. 1978. The status of mute-e. Studies in French Linguistics 1.2, 79–140.
Morin, Y.-C. 1979. La morphophonologie des pronoms clitiques en français populaire. Cahier de linguistique 9, 1–36.
Morin, Y.-C. 1982. De quelques [l] non étymologiques dans le français du Québec: notes sur les clitiques et la liaison. Revue Québécoise de Linguistique 11.2, 9–47.

Morin, Y.-C. 1983. Quelques observations sur la chute du *e* muet dans le français régional de Saint-Étienne. La Linguistique 19.1, 71–93.

Mougeon, R., M. Bélanger, M. Canale and S. Ituen. 1977. L'usage de la préposition SUR en franco-ontarien. Recherches linguistiques à Montréal 8. Canadian Journal of Linguistics 22.2, 95–124.

Nyrop, K. 1930. Grammaire historique de la langue française. 6 vols. Copenhagen: Gyldendals.

Orkin, M. 1967. Speaking Canadian French. Toronto: General Publishing.

Ostiguy, L. 1979. La chute de la consonne *l* dans les articles définis et les pronoms clitiques en français montréalais. Thèse de maîtrise. Université de Montréal.

Paris, G. 1877. *ti*, signe d'interrogation. Romania 6, 438–442.

Pei, M. 1966. Glossary of Linguistic Terminology. New York: Doubleday.

Pernot, H. 1929. Étude phonétique d'un disque canadien. Revue de phonétique appliquée 6, 290–319.

Picard, M. 1974a. L'effacement du schwa dans les monosyllabes en québécois. Cahier de linguistique 4, 1–12.

Picard, M. 1974b. La diphtongue /wa/ et ses équivalents au Canada. Cahier de linguistique 4, 147–155.

Picard, M. 1978. Les voyelles du québécois et l'ordonnance intrinsèque. Cahier de linguistique 7, 71–75.

Picard, M. 1981. Problems in Québécois morphophonology. Innovations in Linguistics Education 2.1, 99–109.

Picard, M. 1983. La productivité des règles phonologiques et les emprunts de l'anglais en québécois. Revue de l'Association québécoise de linguistique 3.2, 97–108.

Pope, M. 1934. From Latin to Modern French with Especial Consideration of Anglo-Norman. Manchester: Manchester UP.

Poplack, S. and D. Walker. 1983. Contraintes sur la variation du *l* en français d'Ottawa-Hull. Paper presented at the 1983 NWAVE conference, Montreal, P.Q.

Poulin, N. 1973. Oral and nasal vowel diphtongization of a New England French dialect. Bruxelles: AIMAV.

Prairie, M. 1976. Sur la structure du mot phonologique en français de Montréal. Thèse de maîtrise. Université du Québec à Montréal.

Price, G. 1971. The French Language: Present and Past. London: Arnold.

Pupier, P. and L. Drapeau. 1973. La réduction des groupes de consonnes finales en français de Montréal. Cahier de linguistique 3, 127–145.

Pupier, P. and F. Grou. 1974. Le [t] final non-standard et les alternances vocaliques du français de Montréal. Cahier de linguistique 4, 57–67.

Pupier, P. and L. Légaré. 1973. L'effacement du /l/ dans les articles définis et les clitiques en français de Montréal. Glossa 7, 63–80.

Pupier, P. and R. Pelchat. 1972. Observations sur la phonologie des pronoms personnels du français de Montréal. Lingua 29, 326–346.

Rigault, A. (ed.) 1971. La grammaire du français parlé. Paris: Hachette.

Robinson, S. and D. Smith. 1979. Manuel pratique du français canadien. Toronto: Macmillan.

Rochette, C. 1972. Consonnes intervocaliques en franco-québécois: étude de phonétique expérimentale. Travaux de linguistique et de littérature 10.1, 225–252.

Rondeau, G., G. Bibeau, G. Gagné and G. Taggart (eds.). 1976. Vingt-cinq ans de linguistique au Canada: hommage à Jean-Paul Vinay. Montréal: CEC.

Rosoff, G. 1974. The function of liaison as a correlate of plurality in spoken French. Canadian Modern Language Review 30, 357–361.

Rousseau, Jacques. 1940. La prononciation canadienne du T et du D. Le Canada français 23, 369–372.

Runte, H. and A. Valdman (eds.). 1976. Identité culturelle et francophonie dans les Amériques II. Bloomington: Indiana University Press.

Sabourin, C. and R. Lamarche. 1979. Le français québécois. Montréal: Office de la langue française.

Sankoff, D. (ed.). 1978. Linguistic Variation. Models and Methods. New York: Academic Press.
Sankoff, D. and H. Cedergren (eds.). 1981. Variation Omnibus. Edmonton: Linguistic Research Inc.
Sankoff, G. and H. Cedergren. 1971a. Some results of a sociolinguistic study of Montreal French. In Linguistic Diversity in Canadian R. Darnell (ed.). Edmonton: Linguistic Research Inc. 61–87.
Sankoff, G. and H. Cedergren. 1971b. Les contraintes linguistiques et sociales de l'élision du (l) chez les Montréalais. Actes du XIIIe Congrès international de linguistique et Philologie romanes.
Sankoff, G. and H. Cedergren. 1972. Sociolinguistic research on French in Montreal. Language in Society I, 173-174.
Santerre, L. 1974. Deux E et deux A phonologiques en français québécois. Cahier de linguistique 4, 117-145.
Santerre, L. 1975. La disparition des voyelles hautes et la coloration consonantique en rapport avec la syllabe, en français québécois. Paper at the 8th International Congress of Phonetic Sciences, Leeds.
Santerre, L. 1976a. Voyelles et consonnes du français québécois populaire. In Valdman 1976, 21-36.
Santerre, L. 1976b. La postériorisation du /a/ en français québécois. Manuscript, Université de Montréal.
Santerre, L. 1976c. Comparaison des /e/ et des /a/ en québécois et en français. In Rondeau et al 1976.
Santerre, L. 1976d. Stabilité et variations des oppositions e/ɛ et a/ɑ en français montréalais. Paper presented at the Canadian Linguistic Association, Quebec, May 1976.
Santerre, L. 1979. Les (r) montréalais en regression rapide. In Lavoie (ed.) 1979, 117-132.
Santerre, L. 1981a. Matrices phonologiques individuelles et variables. In Sankoff and Cedergren (eds.) 1981, 209-214.
Santerre, L. 1981b. Essai de définition du joual. Aspect du français parlé au Québec. Journal of the Atlantic Provinces Linguistic Association 3, 41-50.
Santerre, L. 1982. Des r montréalais imprévisibles et inouïs. Revue québécoise de linguistique 12.1, 77-96.

Santerre, L. and J. Millo. 1978. Diphthongization in Montreal French. In Sankoff (ed.) 1978, 173-184.
Santerre, L., D. Noiseux and L. Ostiguy. 1977. La chute du /l/ dans les articles et les pronoms clitiques en français québécois. In the Fourth Lacus Forum, M. Paradis (ed.), 530-538.
Santerre, L. and L. Ostiguy. 1978. La micro-mélodie à la frontière des mots. Communication à l'ACFAS.
Santerre, L. and D. Villa-Tremblay. 1976. Importance sociolinguistique de la diphtongaison en français montréalais. Communication à l'ACFAS, Sherbrooke.
Santerre, L. and D. Villa. 1979. Les paramètres acoustiques en frontière de mots. In Léon and Rossi 1979, 3-10.
Santerre, L. and P.S. Dufour. 1983. Production et perception des voyelles hautes. Paper presented at the 1983 NWAVE conference, Montreal, P.Q.
Schane, S. 1968. French Phonology and Morphology. Cambridge, Mass.: MIT Press.
Schane, S. 1973. Generative Phonology. Englewood Cliffs: Prentice-Hall.
Selkirk, E.O. 1972. The Phrase Phonology of English and French. Ph.D. Dissertation. MIT.
Seutin, E. 1975. Description grammaticale du parler de l'Ile-aux-Coudres. Montréal: Presses de l'Université de Montréal.
Société du Parler français au Canada. 1930. Glossaire du parler français au Canada. Québec: Action Sociale.
Sommerstein, A. 1977. Modern Phonology. London: Edward Arnold.
Squair, J. 1888. A Contribution to the study of the Franco-Canadian dialect. Proceedings of the Canadian Institute 6, 161-168.
Sturm, M. 1932. Quelques remarques sur la prononciation de la lettre A dans la région de Québec. Le Canada français 19, 844-852.
Taylor, D. and R. Clement. 1974. Normative reactions to styles of Quebec French. Anthropological Linguistics 16.5, 202-217.
Thibault, P. (ed.) 1979. Le français parlé. Études socio-linguistiques. Edmonton: Linguistic Research Inc.

Thogmartin, C. 1974. The phonology of three varieties of French in Manitoba. Orbis 23.2, 335–349.

Thomas, A. 1982. Variations sociophonétiques du français parlé à Sudbury (Ontario). Ph.D. Dissertation. University of Toronto.

Tousignant, C. 1978. La liaison consonantique en français de Montréal. Mémoire de maîtrise. Université de Montréal.

Tousignant, C. and D. Sankoff. 1979. Aspects de la compétence productive et réceptive: la liaison à Montréal. In Thibault (ed.), 1979.

Tousignant, C. and L. Santerre. 1978. Les liaisons comme marques sociolinguistiques en français montréalais. Communication au 46e Congrès de l'ACFAS.

Tranel, B. 1981a. Concreteness in Generative Phonology. Evidence from French. Berkeley: University of California Press.

Tranel, B. 1981b. The treatment of French liaison. Proceedings of the Tenth Anniversary Symposium on Romance Languages, 261–282. Seattle: University of Washington.

Valdman, A. (ed.). 1972. Papers in Linguistics and Phonetics in Memory of Pierre Delattre. The Hague: Mouton.

Valdman, A. 1976a. Introduction to French Phonology and Morphology. Rowley, Mass.: Newbury House.

Valdman, A. (ed.). 1976b. Identité culturelle et francophonie dans les Amériques I. Québec: Presses de l'Université Laval.

Van Ameringen, A. 1978. La liaison dans le français de Montréal. M.A. Thesis. UQAM.

Van Ameringen, A. and H.J. Cedergren. 1981. Observations sur la liaison en français de Montréal. In Sankoff and Cedergren (eds.) 1981, 141–149.

Villa, D. 1977. Fusion des voyelles aux frontières de mots en français québécois. Ph.D. Dissertation. Université de Montréal.

Vinay, J.-P. 1950. Bout de la langue ou fond de la gorge. French Review 23, 489–498.

Vinay, J.-P. 1955. Aperçu des études de phonétique canadienne. Société du Parler français au Canada. Études sur le parler français au Canada, 61–82. Québec: Presses de l'Université Laval.

Vinay, J.-P. 1973. Le français en Amérique du nord: problèmes et réalisations. Current Trends in Linguistics 10. Linguistics in North America, T. Sebeok (ed.). The Hague: Mouton, 323–406.

Vincent, D. and D. Sankoff. 1978. The geographical dimension of phonological variation within an urban speech community (NWAVE IV). Cahier de recherche de mathématiques appliquées. Rapport n° 524.

Walker, D. 1979. Canadian French. In The Languages of Canada, J. K. Chambers (ed.). Montréal: Didier, 133–167.

Walker, D. 1980. Liaison and rule ordering in Canadian French phonology. Linguisticae Investigationes IV. 1, 217–222.

Walker, D. 1982. On a phonological innovation in French. Journal of the International Phonetic Association 12, 72–77.

Walker, D. 1983. Chain shifts in Canadian French phonology. Lingua 60, 103–114.

Walter, H. 1976. La dynamique des phonèmes dans le lexique français contemporain. Paris: France-Expansion.

Walter, H. 1977a. La phonologie du français. Paris: PUF.

Walter, H. (ed.). 1977b. Phonologie et société. Montréal: Didier.

Warnant, L. 1968. Dictionnaire de prononciation française, 3ᵉ édition. Gembloux: Duculot.

Wittmann, H. 1976. Contraintes linguistiques et sociales dans la troncation du /l/ à Trois-Rivières. Cahier de linguistique 6, 13–22.

Yaeger, M. 1979. Context-determined Variation in Montreal French Vowels. Ph.D. Dissertation. University of Pennsylvania.

Yaeger-Dror, M. 1983. Chain shifting pattern for Montreal French. Paper presented at the 1983 NWAVE conference, Montreal, P.Q.

Yaeger, M., H. Cedergren and D. Sankoff. 1977. Harmonie et conditionnement consonantique dans le système vocalique du français parlé à Montréal. In Walter 1977, 25–34.

Yaeger, M. and W. Kemp. 1977. Stress correlates in Montreal French. 83rd meeting of the Acoustic Society of America, University Park, Pennsylvania.

Achevé d'imprimer
en mars 1985 sur les presses
des Ateliers Graphiques Marc Veilleux Inc.
Cap-Saint-Ignace, Qué.